Craftsmanship and the Michigan Union Carpenter

Craftsmanship and the Michigan Union Carpenter

Philip A. Korth

Bowling Green State University Popular Press
Bowling Green, Ohio 43403

Dedication

In memory of Gustav Henry Korth
1867-1944

Contents

Foreword

The edited oral histories contained in this volume were gathered in 1982 with the financial support of the Michigan Council for the Humanities, Ron Means, Executive Director, and the Michigan State Carpenters' Council, Marv Grisham, Executive Secretary. I wish to recognize that support at the outset, for cooperation between this union and the Michigan Council for the Humanities should encourage other unions to approach their humanities councils for project support that will preserve the history of organized American workers.

Specifically, I wish to encourage the collection and editing of oral histories, for that technique provides a wonderfully rich access to rank and file participation in the union movement. Important parts of worker history are accessible through no other means, for the formal records of unions, like the records of many mass organizations, are too often the dry residue of lively and intense debate. The union movement is about values and not about structure; it is about human relationships and only secondarily about bylaws, rules, and legal precedent. For example, the spirit of craftsmanship does not easily reduce to a set of work rules, although work rules may create a rich, even necessary context for facilitating the exercise of craftsmanship. Although formal agreements certainly have become necessary in defence of the worker's dignity, by themselves such records fail to convey the powerful values that inform them.

This volume is a celebration of dignity and craftsmanship. The union carpenters in this volume were all retired from practicing the trade by the time they granted interviews, but their pride in their skill, in their accomplishments, emanates from every interview. The interviews convey a sense of self, a sense of dignity, and an appreciation of the significance of their work. The reader will find no voices of alienation or despair here. That should be reassuring and even remarkable, for modern industrial culture, almost by design, assails the craftsman's values by shattering a trade's integration and by debasing its practice.

During the past century and a half, machine production has abstracted the craftsman's art into a process accessible to rational analysis and division. Analysis has segmented the craftsman's holistic activity into a series of steps performed by machines tended by workers whose

ix

entire attention must focus on the machine's actions. Sometimes, as in the case of a punch press, inattention can imperil the worker, threatening fingers, hands, even lives. Such workers dare not think holistically, and thus they become alienated from the whole process and from the product. That is the modern reality, the context in which we should hear the voices of the carpenters who speak through this book, a context that makes what they say all the more remarkable.

It is important to hear their voices precisely. They do not lament the passing of a Golden Age of craftsmanship, nor declare that everything has gone downhill since steam power first drove the weaver's loom. The old tools and the old methods, they assert, were sufficient to their time, but would be out of place today. These carpenters accept modern ways, and do not yearn openly or secretly for the challenge of wood block planes. The router is their preferred tool, and dressed lumber far more attractive than rough cut.

Carpenters are alert to better ways to do their work, and so inherently view it critically. An old carpenter's adage advises: "Measure twice, cut once." Measuring, calculating, recalculating to find the most efficient, best approach, probably saves them from the clutches of an outworn past, and guides them to creative use of new tools and techniques, all in the service of craftsmanship.

The craftsmanship involved in putting this volume together called for measuring twice, and a lot of cutting. The materials from which it was constructed came in a large measure from carpenters themselves. The primary principle that guided my cutting and pasting rested upon my desire to facilitate the story these craftsmen wished to tell. My tools were at their service.

I had help in keeping the cuts precise and the tools sharp by my colleagues in the Gang of Four: Dr. Reed Baird, Dr. Bruce Curtis, and Dr. James McClintock, masters in their own right at crafting with words. I owe them much for their insights, suggestions, and support. Brothers in the union movement, Anthony O'Chocki and Harold McCastle, offered encouragement and useful suggestions.

This volume, which reviews the past, is also a guide to the future, for the craftsmanship these interviews convey, assures that carpentry will be practiced for ages to come. In decades hence we will surely find carpenters amid sawdust and shavings plying their trade.

Philip A. Korth

Introduction

As portions of Michigan began to emerge from the wilderness and show signs of permanent settlement by Europeans, as the need to have things plumb, level and square asserted itself, an itinerant carpenter certainly appeared, carting behind him the chest he had made to protect the tools of his trade. The record of his presence in Michigan appears in art and artifact, from simple family dwellings to Renaissance Center, from waterfront docks and piers to the ships tied up to them, from sash-and-door mills to factories making pre-fabricated houses, from the simple country bridge spanning the Titabawassee River to the magnificent Mackinac Bridge spanning the Straits of Mackinac. The work of the carpenter is diverse and complex, reflecting both technological evolution in the trade and the craftsman's adaptability.

This volume presents Michigan union carpenters' recollections of the past eighty years, recorded as oral histories, and thus offers insights into the meaning of craftsmanship. Work plays such an important role in establishing identity in American culture, that some would say it defines the person. Puritans named it one's calling, and linked it with their performance of God's will. Today it may no longer carry this religious burden, but without question it continues to locate a person in society. We teach our children its importance when we ask them "What are you going to be when you grow up?" We do not expect them to respond: "A kind, warm, sensitive human being," although that might fervently be hoped. Rather, we expect them to identify work they intended to perform; and we can all remember the question and our early answers: policeman, fireman, nurse, doctor, pilot. Each was an answer an adult could accept. The lesson we learned was: *you are your work.* So it is that in American culture, when we examine perceptions of work, we discover much more than technique. We discover how we locate ourselves in our world.

These recorded recollections also allow us to celebrate the skill and adaptability of the union carpenter, as he confronted and mastered evolutions in the tools, methods, and materials he used in the practice of his trade. Many operations performed by hand four score years ago are performed by machines now. Wood has given way to metals and synthetic materials. Each change presented a challenge to the carpenter individually and collectively. Despite a strong sense of independence, carpenters early on recognized the need for collective action in order to preserve their individual autonomy. The craft of carpentry in Michigan, as in other parts of the country, includes the craft union, developed by Michigan carpenters as early as the 1830s to defend their interests and promote high standards in the trade. The work and the union flowed naturally together.

We begin this story with these two most essential experiences underpinning their craftsmanship: becoming a carpenter and joining the union. These experiences define the men interviewed for this study: all are carpenters and members of the United Brotherhood of Carpenters and Joiners of America.

Chapter I
Becoming a Carpenter

[A carpenter] was nailing up siding on a house, and every once in a while, he'd throw the nail away. The foreman came along and said, "What are you throwing them nails away for? Don't you know you're wasting nails?"

"Well," the carpenter said, "the head is on the wrong end."

"You're supposed to hang on to them," the foreman replied. "We use them on the inside."

Wilbur Slye, Escanaba Local 1832

Almost a century ago, carpenters in Pittsburg, Kansas, Local 646, investigated the origins of the term *carpenter* in order to define the carpenter's work. They shared their discovery and definition with *The Carpenter*, the national publication of the United Brotherhood of Carpenters and Joiners.

Strictly speaking, a carpenter is one who constructs the framework of a house, ship or bridge, made of wood. The carpenter completes whatever is necessary to make the structure substantial. The house-carpenter completes the framework of the outside wall and of the partitions; he also completes the roof and the floor. Whatever is *joined on* to the *frame* of the house by way of finishing or ornament, made of wood, belongs to the *joiner*. The joiner also makes the doors, sash, stairs, mantels, stationary cupboards, closets, and puts in place the facing, washboard or baseboard, and whatever else is necessary to complete the woodwork of the house. . . .

Wood, above all else, united these craftsmen, and the work the Kansas local defined fits well with our general understanding of carpentry, but the definition is deceptively simple, for carpentry now, and probably even then, involves much more complex processes. The origins of the term suggests that complexity, for it comes from the Old French which referred to wagon or carriage makers. Today, a member of the United Brotherhood of Carpenters and Joiners may build bridge footings; drive piling; install lathe; build fiberglass boats, and fishing rods; build cupboards; dive in full deep-sea gear; build sky-scrapers and even houses. Wood, metals, concrete, plastics, all take shape under modern, power-driven tools guided by a carpenter's hand. The adaptability which transformed a wagon maker into a house carpenter, led the house carpenter into cabinet making and even dressed him in deep sea diving gear.

3

That adaptability emerges through the personal narratives of Michigan carpenters whose paths to carpentry as a trade were sometimes most indirect. Today's carefully organized apprenticeship schools sponsored by the UBCJA and contractors, educate students in the principles, practices and tricks of the trade. Modern institutions, they respond to a traditional desire to protect and preserve high quality workmanship in the trade. Such schools have not always been available to those who wished to enter the trade. Some carpenters, following ancient tradition, carry on the family trade, having learned it at their fathers' workbenches. Others become carpenters in less traditional ways. Carpenters tell an old story with variations, about the apprentice who lost his balance and fell four stories to the ground. A journeyman carpenter ran up and with furrowed brow asked, "what happened?" The apprentice replied, "I don't know. I just got here myself."

Not everyone entered the trade accidentally, of course, but some recall becoming a carpenter with some amazement, if not wonder. Their answer to the question "How did you get into carpentry?" revealed the diversity of backgrounds and circumstances that brought workers into this trade. We begin with the formal entrance.

Jake Michel, Saginaw Local 334:

I finished school in 1912 and worked four years at Saginaw Manufacturing Company which made wood split pulleys and washboards. I couldn't be an apprentice until I was 16. I was getting 10 cents an hour and working steady 54 hours a week. I got $5.40 a week. And they were going to raise me to 12 cents an hour. They said I would be sorry if I quit, but I quit anyway. I wanted to be a carpenter. Dad was a cabinet maker, but when he came here to Michigan [from Russia in 1907] he followed construction—mostly finishing. He wasn't no form builder; he was a carpenter and he taught me the trade.

I had my apprenticeship with Fred C. Trier. He was a craftsman, he come up the line too. My dad worked for him too. I learned my trade from [Trier]. I was indentured to him April 20, 1916. My dad signed off and I couldn't work for nobody but him. The indenture was for three years and at the end of that three years he was the one who decided whether you were capable, whether he would pay you the carpenters' rate. He had that prerogative. You had to work another year if you didn't come up to standard. [The indenture] was the old style way of binding someone. It was not used too long after 1916.

Jake Michel, Saginaw Local 334

Elmer Swanson, Escanaba Local 1832:

My father was a carpenter. Seems like I was always a carpenter. I only went through the 8th grade and I started working with my dad right away. I served my apprenticeship under him. There was no formal apprenticeship in them days. Usually it was a father and son deal. Once in a while a contractor would take in a relative or a friend.

Kenneth Johnson, Muskegon Local 100:

My father was a carpenter. When things got rough [during the Depression] he went off building houses for himself, and he couldn't see my laying around, so that's how it worked in. I served an apprenticeship here. They didn't have stuff like they have today, the school and all. You just did. You worked for less and you worked so long. They laid things out and you sawed them by hand. Nothing was pre-cut.

Vincent Kowalski, Mt. Clemens Local 674:

I came to Mt. Clemens in the Air Corps in 1934 and served my hitch. I got out to seek employment and started in an automobile factory in '37. I couldn't stand the inside. My family is carpenters from way back; my dad and all his brothers, and all my brothers, except two out of seven, are carpenters. So it just seemed to fall in that line, that's all. I was around carpentry ever since I was a kid. I started in carpentry when the CCC was in business. I was in the CCC for about a year and was the company carpenter. That was my first responsibility as a carpenter.

Walter L. Weir, Mt. Clemens Local 674:

I was milking cows and 5 o'clock was milking time and I was a minute late. That was brought up at the breakfast table at 6 o'clock. So I just quit. My daddy was a carpenter all his life, so I come home and he said "what are you doing here?" And that following morning I went to work with him. That was how I got started. This was in the 30s.

The choice to carry on the family tradition may not have been free. It may not have been a choice at all. The father's role as teacher, so clear in the lives of Jake Michel and Elmer Swanson, may have been less direct in other cases.

Merlin Veysey Sault Ste. Marie Local 46:

I grew up here in the Soo until I was about 18. I left the Soo and went to Flint. The [First World] War was just getting over then and we didn't have nothing. There wasn't no work for anybody, so the young fellows of that day had to go where they could find the work. I was

Elmer Swanson, Escanaba Local 1832

one of them that went down to Flint. I worked and put up a big building 200 by 300 feet doing carpentry work there. It was a parts building [for Buick]. Before that I worked for my father who was a carpenter. He was one of those carpenters that: "If you're going to do it, do it and don't ask me how to do it." He was an old time carpenter. He gave you a job and you better figure it out and do it. He wouldn't tell you about nothing. He was a carpenter from Canada. His dad didn't teach him either. So you make up your mind to do something and you do it. That's just the way I learned.

M.H. "Buck" Huber, Clearwater Local 2026:

Originally, my dad was a carpenter, but he got so he didn't want to do anything. I grew up on farm, did some logging and some rodeoing. When there wasn't any carpentry work going on, I would get back to rodeoing. I had to quit school after the seventh grade to help support my parents and my brothers and sisters. I had done some barn building helping some old fellows around. I started reading some veterinary books. My grand dad was an old veterinarian. So, whenever I needed some groceries real bad, I'd sharpen up my jack-knife and make the rounds and castrate stallions, bulls, boars, rams, anything they had that they wanted that done to. In them times, you just had to study a lot of different ways of getting in a couple dollars here and there. This was mostly through the thirties.

Mostly [I learned] by bluff. Man say, "have you ever done so and so?" I'd say, "that's the only thing I ever done!" About noon he'd come a long and see that I hadn't told it just exactly straight. He might just feel enough for me to keep me on, or he might just can me right then and there. But I had a little experience and the next job would last just a little bit longer. I'd just pick it up here and there, the best way there was. There was a lot of bluffing to it.

Roman Dunneback, Lansing Local 1449:

I was a butcher. I worked in a slaughterhouse quite a lot, but my father was an old time German, and he was a hard man to get along with. He was a perfectionist. He had every [carpenter's] tool that was made. He said it took eight years for an apprenticeship when he went in. He was everything. He was jack of all trades and a master of all trades. I'm jack of all trades and master of darn few of them. The breeze blew between us a little bit hard, you know. There was 13 of us and I was down there about number 11 where they get a bit disgusted, you know. I decided that I had to get into something [other than butchering] because it was paying only $22 a week for 60 hours. I was about 24. It was 1927. My oldest brother was a blacksmith and my next brother worked with my father a lot as carpenters. I could go with my brother, but he wasn't much easier to get along with than my father, but I always thanked the good Lord that [I went with him], because he did a lot of diversified work and it got me into a lot of diversified work. I became a handy man, I could do everything because he did everything.

Whether one learned from his father, or despite his father, the lessons fell on fertile ground. A feeling for the work, for the materials imply an instinct, an intuitive sense that carpentry was the right trade.

Sylvester "Wes" Hellner, Mt. Clemens Local 674:

In the early days I was working at the Mt. Clemens pottery making dishes. I made enough dishes to go from here to the moon. It was seven years. The [Second World] War was beginning to stir up in Europe. I had a low number and I was drafted. I got in the Air Force. The age limit was 35 and they lowered it down to 28. Well I was already thirty, and I was entitled to get out. After I got out my dad asked the business agent if I could get a job somewhere. He said yeah go down to Cramer Homes. My dad went down there too. These living quarters for war workers needed coal bins. They build them on the outside. This foreman said "I'll tell you what we want done."

When he left I says to my dad, "What the hell is he talking about anyway?" So my dad started to explain a little bit. I said, "Is that all he's talking about? Let's go to work!" In an hour I knew how to build that dumb thing.

As far as learning the trade, I always thought there was nothing to it. When I was sixteen—about 1925, '26—my dad decided to put an addition on the house. In the morning before he went to work, he says, "well, I want this done, and that done." I'd say okay. And when he came home at night it was done. In a week's time we had the addition on and I did all the work. I could visualize it. I never had any trouble visualizing something done. It just come natural.

Cornelius Vos, Muskegon Local 100:

I had a permit to work when I was fifteen years old. My dad got one for me instead of me going to school. I had to go to work when I was 16. But by that time I had worked. [When I was] between 12 and 13 years old I had worked all summer long on a house my dad was building.

[My dad] was a cabinet maker. He always worked in the furniture factories. As soon as my dad got enough money to build that house, why I was the first guy that was going to do it, see. I was only a kid, but I was a big shot, see.

When he hired a carpenter to build that house, I was right there on the spot, seven o'clock in the morning, just like the carpenter, and working all day long. I really took interest in carpentry work right from the start. Right from the start I always liked wood. When I was a kid I was always hunting for a piece of wood to make a kite out of, or something like that. My first job, in the Racine Boat Company, we had a big boat to build there and we had Michigan White Pine for the deck. I took home a piece and I have a chain carved out of wood each link separately, over three feet long with a ball on one end and a hook on the other. So you see that come natural to me. Always wood. Nothing but wood.

The first carpenter that interested me in fancy work, was a crippled guy, but he took a fancy to kids—I must have been about 22 years old. He showed me how to build a stairway. I never forgot that. I could build a stairway on a circle or going up and I would come out [exact]. After that I got in with a house carpenter. What I didn't know he'd show me.

Ray Skiba, Alpena Local-1132:

It pretty much ran in the family. My dad was a carpenter. My brother Tony, he was a contractor. Outside of plumbing, the family has had just about every trade that was in the construction business. In construction you usually had extra help so we pretty much all got experience in the construction business and mostly in the carpentry business.

Surely, some sons of carpenters did not become carpenters, and just as certainly, some carpenters do not trace the trade back through the family. Circumstance, conditions and people, the accidents of time and place, could determine the path one might take, and lead one into the trade.

Roy Bade, Mt. Clemens Local 674:

I was working in a lumber yard in New Baltimore at $17 a week in '39 or '40. I wanted more money and he couldn't afford to pay it. My neighbor and his brother who lived in Detroit were building houses. I got to talking to them and they said, yeah, they'd give me a job, so that's how I got started. My grand dad was a carpenter, but I had never really worked with him. In those days, you just worked in as you went along.

Ray Skiba, Alpena Local 1132

Wilbur Slye, Escanaba Local 1832:

When the end of the War came this company [I worked for] went into the wood door business with a door company. They made steel doors for airport hangers and stuff like that. Then they made wooden doors, and so I went to work in the wood door division, and then I went on the road for them installing these wood doors. I put all them wood doors in the Chevrolet plants in Flint, the Chrysler plants. These are twenty-four feet wide; these doors weighed tons and [used] electric operators. Because I went out in the field installing doors, I had to join the Carpenters' Union because I run into these construction jobs where they were union.

Grady Pinner, Berkley Local 998:

My first job was honey dipping—cleaning septic tanks. When I went to high school I worked at a gas station after school and weekends—Saturdays, we didn't work Sundays in those days.

We didn't have any formal carpentry education. I learned it the hard way: On the job. I had an old fellow by the name of Joe Robertoy who was a carpenter, and I used to go around with him once in a while after school and on Saturdays and he had a Model T Ford and we rode out to the job in a Model T. We built garages and I helped him several times. I kinda like the smell of sawdust. This is the middle thirties. When I was drafted into the army [during World War II] I had some carpentry experience so they made a carpenter out of me there, strange as it may seem. At one point I had a carpentry shop in the army and did repairs, and built items that was needed.

Ezell Johnson, Battle Creek Local 871:

I was raised on a farm [in Tennessee]. Back when I was about 15 years old I used to work around with a guy that belonged to our church by the name of Arthur Manning. He was a journeyman carpenter and after school and during the summer he always had some work for me. It was just part of his feeling to help, mostly youngsters, but anyone. He seemed to cater to boys who acted like they wanted to advance in life. I didn't know if that little dib-dabbing would amount to anything. That's why I didn't start with it when I moved to Illinois. I just got whatever work I could get.

At that time, down there a real estate man hired on a guy to take care of all of his houses, to do the repair work, and he was a journeyman carpenter. I thought about carpentry work when they began talking about the war. I heard my uncle talk about in every war how they would build. Then my mind run back to the experience I had in building. I said, I believe I'd like to go back. Then here came this guy, "You seem like a nice fellow and haven't been married long. I've got a job taking care

Ezel Johnson, Battle Creek Local 871

of a lot of houses and I'm pretty well behind in my work and I'm getting older too. How about you coming in working with me. I'll treat you right. I notice you are working nights (I was working from 12 to 6 a.m. He lived right across the street from me.). Seems to me that you are kinda ambitious."

I said, "I can always use a little bit more work." Right then I got tied in with him.

The path to carpentry also ran through the school shop where one developed skills making book ends, coffee tables and desks under the watchful eye of a teacher.

Ralph Haines, Battle Creek Local 871:

I took four years of manual training. We'd cure the wood on top of the old coal furnace. We had to learn to sharpen tools. The teacher's name was P.D. Ellspaugh. When I got out of high school I went to work in the engineering department of the Briscoe Automobile factory in Jackson. I went from there to the Hayes Wheel Company where we were involved with hickory in making the wheel spokes. From there I went to work for Cooper Brothers contractors building houses.

My brother and I started in doing that. And we had to do everything from laying the stone wall to putting on the wood lathe. I liked to work with wood so I liked the trade. We learned to plaster, we learned to lay stone, we learned to lay brick, all on our own. The two men we worked for were all-round carpenters. They did everything.

Of the forces that might lead one to carpentry as a trade, necessity infused them all. Only through work, remunerative work, could one put food on the table and maintain respectability. Carpentry was simply one way.

Ed Harper, Berkley Local 998:

I came from Illinois up to Pontiac there and [carpentry] was about the only thing I could get work at. J.A. Eddly was building the Fisher body plant, so I went to work for him. I just picked it up looking over other fellows' shoulders on that Fisher Body plant job.

Michael J. Sammon, Detroit Local 337:

My father was a farmer. He died pretty young: sixty four. We didn't have much of an apprenticeship program. We used to work with carpenters. That's where we learned our trade, the old timers, anyway. I just loved to work around as a carpenter, building a house. [My first house,] I was out for crops in western Canada, but I was there too early,

Michael Sammon, Detroit Local 337

and this fellow came along and said, "you want a job?" He said it was not in the fields, because the grain is not ready yet. He said, "I'm starting to build a house out on some property I have. You want to come out there and help me?" We went out there and I never saw him for a week. I didn't know what the hell I was doing, you know. He later set stairs for me and said put them together so we can get to the second floor. He was a good guy. We got the second floor up and that's where I slept. The next day in the morning I didn't have breakfast 'til he come. I'd be doing something when he come, 'cause he wouldn't get there [with breakfast] 'til nine o'clock. Building a house for some farmer.

Ed Cooper, Traverse City Local 1461:

The first contractor I worked for was a mason. He carried a card as a bricklayer. He had two sons who were bricklayers and one son who done the office work. He came from Sweden and brought the knowledge with him and he set up business here in Traverse City. You started out by being just a handy man, doing a little bit of everything. I know I done lots and lots of cement work. I never really cared that much about [bricklaying]. You know you'd look at your fingers and they was always worn down to the nubs. I was always able to do it, but as a profession I didn't care too much for it. I always liked to work with wood. A pretty piece of wood is something I always liked, just the color of the wood, the grain in it and the things you could do with it.

A love of wood, a desire to shape and mould it brought many to the craft of carpentry, but new materials and new processes altered or displaced traditional methods and practices. The smell of sawdust, memorable, distinct, gave way to other smells. Hardwood floors have virtually disappeared, replaced by carpet, tile, linoleum and other synthetic materials. Those who laid hardwood flooring have been replaced by workers skilled in handling the new materials.

Michael Belles, Detroit Resilient Floor Local 2265:

I come out here [in 1925] and got a job with the American Metal Products Company, cutting exhaust pipes and steering gear jackets. I worked piece work and I made $100 in two weeks, which was a tremendous amount of money at that time. Within a month's time they cut me down so I worked just as hard for fifty. So I quit and went back to Pennsylvania. After about six months, I came back out here and went to work for Western Waterproofing Company, waterproofing brick joints and basements, supervising the installation of drain tile on both sides of the footing. Then, of course, that was seasonal work. In the wintertime you were out of work. I stayed with that until about 1938 when I got into laying tile at the Brewster Housing for a Chicago firm. That was one of the first Federal low cost housing that was put in this area. I was laying tile then with a Cement Finishers card.

David Charlton, Detroit Resilient Floor Local 2265:

I was born in Canada and came here in 1926. I started to work at Carlton-Millers as a carpet worker. I was 18. I worked there until 1932. Then the fellow who had run the linoleum department started a business out on Dexter Boulevard and he asked me to go out there with him. And I did as a carpet layer.

Bill Potter, Detroit Resilient Floor Local 2265:

I come here from Bay City when I was 16 years old and I got a job at Crowley's driving truck. I had nine years in over there [when I quit]. The boss wanted to see me before I left. So I went up and seen him and he said, "What are you throwing nine years over your shoulder for?"

I said, "I can't get along with that so-and-so-over there."

He said, "How would you like to learn to lay linoleum?"

I says, "That's union. I can't get in there."

He says, "You know the guy who runs the carpet work room?" Go up and see him."

So I went up there and the fellow said, "Yeah, Bill, we need an apprentice. Come in in the morning and see the Steward." So I come in and he said, "Sure, Bill, but first you got to go down and see the Business Agent." The Business Agent told me, "Sure, but first you go back and tell them to give you a letter where I can go into that carpet work room any time." So I went back there and they give me the letter. [The Business Agent] give me a card and the next morning I went back to work at Crowley's.

L.M. "Boots" Weir, Detroit Millwright Local 1102:

I grew up on a farm. I came here by way of St. Louis. I was looking for employment in St. Louis at the Chevrolet plant. I didn't care what type. I had no specific trade in mind. So a man came out and hired me. He represented the Mechanical Handling Systems of Detroit and was there doing a specific conveyor job at the Chevrolet motor plant. He asked me if I knew anything about conveyors and I said nothing but a belt conveyor that I had seen around a saw mill or a gravel separation plant. He said, "Well, you look like you're big enough to earn 40 cents an hour. If you're not you won't last very damn long." So that's how I come to Michigan by way of that company.

Some traditional carpenters' work left the construction site altogether, largely because it lent itself to machine production and industrial methods. Operatives in these industries are often erroneously classified as unskilled and semi-skilled workers; many of them have had formal training.

Ralph Krimmel, Industrial Council, Battle Creek:

I worked in a cabinet shop while I was supporting myself getting through school. While I was doing that I learned something about the trade. [When I moved back to Battle Creek, I] went to the Unemployment to get a job and they sent me out here to Michigan Woodwork which is a custom cabinet making shop and trim company. I went to work for them and served a partial apprenticeship—I got credit for my previous experience—and I became a journeyman cabinet maker and trim man. This was about 1946.

The multitude of skills one developed on the farm could readily prepare one for the trade. Growing up in northern Michigan, clearing land to bring wilderness under cultivation, nurtured the skill to handle one of the carpenter's oldest tools and could lead into the trade through the work of pile driving.

Donald McLeod, Sault Ste. Marie Local 46:

Before my father immigrated to the United States from Canada, he followed the river drives over there. He decided to move to the United States [and became] a farmer on Neebish Island. He ended up with 460 acres of ground down there, practically all cleared. We cleared it. I had three uncles who went down to Toledo to work in factories and mostly in construction. That's how I got started. They said why don't you come down? There's lots of work down here. My dad didn't want me to go. My mother cried and bawled when I left, but my dad slipped me $25.00. When I got there only one was working, but [he] was working in construction, working on a riverfront project on the Cherry Street Bridge.

They were driving a lot of wooden piling. They were having problems keeping enough piling ahead. They had three rigs, driving and they couldn't get [the piles] headed and sharpened fast enough. They were dry, oak piling. We came home from this little job we had at the sugar beet factory one night and he said, "How'd you like to go to work for me in the morning? My boss, Bernie Kelley, wants to hire a couple of good men. I told him I've got two guys from Northern Michigan that was practically raised with an axe in each hand." Some of these piles had to be cut down to 11 inches, a foot back from the face so the hammer would fit on it. Then we had to sharpen the other end. So we went there. It was paying about twice what we were making at the sugar beet factory. So we went down and he gave us a brand new axe and a cant hook to roll them around.

We worked like buggers there for about three or four days. After a couple of days we had a few left over and we kept working 'til we got way ahead of the pile drivers. I worked there until about April. I told Dad that I would be back in the spring, which I did, and I worked on the farm with him and the rest of the family until fall and I went back to Toledo. That was about 1921. I was pretty young then. We worked on two or three railroad overpasses. I worked in pile driving until about 1928 and then I joined the dredgemen for about three years deepening the harbor in the Maumee River. What I learned, I learned on the job. I was very aggressive on the job, I was a bugger to work. I didn't have a teacher, but you learn a lot working with other men; you pick it up.

The young worker might learn difficult lessons on his way to carpentry. Work experiences in the early twentieth century could still be brutal, threatening health and even life itself. The outrages of nineteenth century industrialism persisted, particularly in hard times. Working conditions and the pace of some industrial jobs could be lethal. In such a context carpentry seemed relatively autonomous and certainly more dignified.

Wilbur Slye, Escanaba Local 1832:

I worked at Buckeye [in Gladstone]. I can remember when everybody had to come to work in the morning and stand there—about a hundred people. The foreman would come over there and point, you and you, because he had notice from the Buckey store that you owed a bill and the only way you could get work there was to owe in the company store. If you owed a bill in the company store, then you had work. When payday came, you got a pink slip. My father had a large family, and he was getting around fifteen cents an hour. If one of the boys could work, he'd go over there and help pay the bill. So I worked at this to help supplement my father's wages.

This was about '27, '28. I went to work at the paper mill. They paid me 24 cents an hour, and it was seven days a week and when you wanted to take your girl friend out, you had to work a sixteen hour shift, in order to get a day off. I can remember standing up to that machine, they called it a wet machine, and the pulp came over this machine and they balled it up and shipped it out to other companies. I can still remember being half asleep and walking from one machine to another. Then I advanced to a different department and I worked in a beater room. We tried to keep up with that paper machine. I remember

Wilbur Sly, Escanaba Local 1832

one time the superintendent said to me: "What's the matter with you that you can't keep up with that paper machine?"

I said, "There's no man alive can keep up with them!"

He said, "If you don't like it, there's five hundred men out there to take your place." And there was!

Many's the day I carried my lunch pail home because I didn't have time to eat. The guys who worked in the paper mill didn't have the brains of a fly, because at night the fly flew up to the ceiling and went to sleep, while the guys in the paper mills went to work.

Cornelius Vos, Muskegon Local 100:

My first real job to earn my money was in the sawmill at ten cents an hour. One guy was pushing it through the rip saw and I was piling it up. I can never forget the first day. You had to be to work at seven o'clock. It was ten hours a day. This guy says to me, "What time do you thing it is?" We had started at seven o'clock.

I says, "It must be pretty near twelve o'clock."

"Huh," he says. "We stop at nine o'clock for coffee. They haven't told us to go yet."

Merlin Veysey, Sault Ste. Marie Local 46:

The first carpenter job I got here [in the Soo after I returned from Flint] was with Irv Lawson. That's back in '35, '36. I asked him for a job.

He asked, "Are you a carpenter?"

I said, "I don't know. I done a little bit."

He said, "you come in tomorrow morning and bring your tools with you. If I think you earned your day's wages tomorrow, I'll give you thirty five cents an hour." They put me to work with his partner, siding one house. We run up the gable end of that house, from the ground, walked around the other side and went up as far as the eave. Two men on the back didn't quite make the gable...I found out I was crazy, working that hard. Years back, you'd get up in the morning and go to work and [the contractor] said, "there's a fifty pound keg of nails there. Drive them before you go home tonight." He meant it. That's a lot of nails.

These carpenters, from "Buck" Huber who learned by bluff, to "Boots" Weir who parlayed his size into becoming a mill wright, to Elmer Swanson whose father brought him into the trade, took the risks, made their mistakes, and learned, largely by doing. How quintessentially American. It is almost gilding the lily to note in some the mysterious workings of affinity, drawing them gently to work in wood.

Chapter II
Joining the Union

The [carpenter] did some work for a lawyer and handed him a bill for two hundred dollars. The lawyer said, "I can't make that kind of money, and I'm a lawyer."
The carpenter replied, "Neither could I when I was a lawyer."

Grady Pinner, Berkley Local 998

The centuries old practice of creating trades unions has established, not surprisingly, a tradition of union membership among working people. That tradition rests upon a practical and often skeptical analysis of a union's advantages. One follows that tradition because it works. And like any other tool the carpenter employs, utility measures its worth, even when the tool is handed from father to son.

Elmer Swanson, Escanaba Local 1832:

My father was a union man, oh, yes, oh yes. I have never missed a month's dues in all those sixty some years. Never missed a month's dues. In the [Great] Depression, I paid my father's dues. The old mechanics, they wanted to belong to the union, which my father was, and he wouldn't miss a meeting on a bet. They were real good mechanics, all of them. They were all old men. There was no young fellows at all. There were 62 members. The way it was set up in the union, you would explain to them that you were taking in a 14 year old as an apprentice. Whenever the contractor or your father or whoever you were learning your trade from would notify the union that you were a full-fledged mechanic and you were 18 years old, then you would get your card. I was pretty proud the day I got it. They were very strict.

George Elliott, Detroit Local 19:

I joined the union in 1937. Raymond [Construction Company] had a union contract. During the Depression there was no union anyplace, except here in Detroit and Cincinnati, Ohio. I think [the union] was a little bit born into me. My grandfather that raised me was a veterinarian from Scotland and he came to this country around 1880. He taught at Alfred University in the veterinary school for 36 years. He believed in unions. They had a union at that school for teachers. He used to tell

1890 Labor Day Parade Float, Local 100, Muskegon, Mich. (Courtesy Muskegon County Museum).

George Elliott, Detroit Piledrivers' Local 19

me when I was young kid, 8, 9, 10 years old, "George, whatever you do, if you have to work for a living, belong to a union." It was drilled into me and I just believed in it. To this day, I don't think there is anything for a working man better than a union.

Kenneth Johnson, Muskegon Local 100.
[My father] joined the union in 1907, Local 100. Seven dollars initiation fee. Once in a while I went with him to union meetings [when I was a kid] to the hall down there on Western Avenue.

Sylvester "Wes" Hellner, Mt. Clemens Local 674:
My father was Financial Secretary of the local.

Jacob Michel, Saginaw Local 334:
My dad was a good union man and he worked a lot with Bill Hutchenson [President of the UBCJA from 1915 to 1952.] here nights and Sundays. You worked six days a week, at that time. That goes back to Russia. I lost my German language on account of him. He said, "We are in America and we're going to speak the American language." In the old country they were taking everything away from him, so when he came to this country and was able to join an organization, [he] worked for its betterment because of the treatment they had got in the old country. They had the same treatment around here—not that bad, maybe, but if you worked for a certain wage and some other guy would work for less, well you was out of a job. That's why it was easier to get a guy to join a union, so he would have an equal chance.

Before I was allowed to go to work, I joined the union as an apprentice. I enjoyed working for Fred Trier. He was a man that knew his business. He was a good union man. He was president of our local when he started contracting. First there were two brothers and they both belonged to the union. The one I worked for, Fred, was president of local 334. He had to relinquish his card. He couldn't carry a card and be a contractor. The contractor handled the apprentice. You were a member of the local but you were indentured to the contractor and that's the only one you worked for. At the end of three years, you had a meeting of the union and the contractor, and the contractor said you're okay and you got your journeyman's card. Then you paid the rest of your initiation fees.

Everybody who worked together had a card. Every Monday morning you showed your card, and if you was behind and had no good reason like sickness, or laid off, you went down that night and paid your month's dues. Every Monday morning everybody showed their card to everybody else. You didn't show it to just one man. Every Monday: "Here's my card. Where's yours?" They didn't have to have somebody run around [and check]. We was too tickled to get a decent wage and decent working conditions created by belonging to the union. Today, a carpenter must be a union member to work on a union job.

Roy Bade, Mt. Clemens Local 674:

I joined the union in 1941. I was out looking and happened to see this job, and I stopped in and asked about a job and they said: "You've got to join the union."

"Where do I join the union." They told me to go to Detroit, so I went down there and inquired and they told me there was one here [in Mt. Clemens], so that's where I joined. In fact I signed up in [Wes's] father's basement. He had an office there.

Vincent Kowalski, Mt. Clemens Local 674:

My first job was the filtration plant up at Marysville. He says, "Have you got a card?"

I says, "No."

"Well," he says, "You'll have to get a card. You'll have to take an examination." So I went up there and they had examining for people from the Local to see if you knew. So I qualified. That was in 1938.

Roy Bade, Mt. Clemens Local 674:

It was a little different experience [for me]. There was an apprentice program of some kind, I don't remember what it was. I had my choice. [They asked me,] "Do you want to go into an apprenticeship program?"

I said, "no, I just want to be a member."

"You'll have to take a test."

"That's fine with me." So I paid, so much a week. Finally I got all paid up and went to a meeting.

They said, "Well, what are we going to do with these fellows?" (Seemed like about six of us.)

"Well, We'll initiate 'em."

"Well, what about the examination?"

"We'll send them down afterwards and give them their money back if they don't pass." Shortly after that, I got laid off. I went out to Ypsilanti to the bomber plant and I cleared into the Ann Arbor Local. During that period, it was just forgot about. I just kinda missed the examination.

M.H. "Buck" Huber, Coldwater Local 2026:

Along about '47 or '48, I made a little down payment on initiation out in Iowa and that job didn't last very long. When I came back up

M.H. "Buck" Huber, Coldwater Local 2026

here, I joined the Coldwater local and I have been in ever since. The job in Iowa was organized. I had to belong there to work.

Donald McLeod, Sault Ste. Marie Local 46:

In 1929 things were really getting rough. I used to go up to the Union hall and there'd be ten, twelve, fifteen people sitting around there waiting for a call. I didn't like that very well. Some of these guys was nearly ready to retire. Local Union 38 in Toledo the pile drivers and the carpenters were all in one. I never worked on a union job before that job in Toledo. It was necessary [to join the union]. That was a union job. They give you so long to join. The initiation fee was very small. When I came to the Soo in 1942, I had been away from the construction work for quite some time and I had to re-join here. It cost me $25.00.

Ralph Haines, Battle Creek Local 871:

In 1923, '24 they built the Michigan State Prison, the largest prison in the world. The day after I hired on, I was elected Business Agent for the Carpenters' Union. Jackson Local 74. That was the first union for me.

The great organizing drives of the 1930s which created the large industrial unions of the C.I.O. also stimulated growth among craft unions, for they created an atmosphere conducive to union organizing. Just as circumstances made some workers into carpenters, so circumstance made some into union supporters, and in the 1930s unionism was in the air.

Grady Pinner, Berkeley Local 998:

In 1937 when those sit down strikes started, I sat down in one of those plants up there with my dad in Pontiac, so I got acquainted [with unions] early. When I graduated from High School in 1937, they were trying to organize the steel workers down there in Monroe. We drove down there one morning—well, late at night. We stayed in our cars and got up and drove into town. They put us all in jail. They had the vigilantes out. American Legion, guys with rags around their arms with ball bats, and shotguns and what-have-you. They turned us loose the next morning and told us not to come back, and I never went back until about five years ago. Beautiful jail outside, lousy inside.

[My dad] was a union man. He got fired out of those auto plants up there for trying to organize the old A.F.L. auto union. This was before the U.A.W. came. We had an early education in picket lines, and violence. We don't like violence, but we saw it. I saw state police and

Ralph Haines, Battle Creek Local 871

machine guns set up in front of the plants. It was rough. It was rougher working without the union, though. They got organized because there was a need for it.

I got drafted into the service. There were union carpenters on the post. I remember there was guys from local 54 in Louisville and I worked in conjunction with them. I joined the Carpenters in 1945, two weeks after I got out of the military. I got a pass just before I got discharged and I came home and went to work for a contractor up in Pontiac, named Forsythe. I worked for him two or three days and he said, "When you get back, you come and look me up. I'll put you to work." So I did. I worked for him about two or three days and he said, "Now I want you to get down there in Birmingham and join the union. I don't want old man Lumley out here stomping around my job, tearing my job up." So I went down and joined the union October 19, 1945. I've been there ever since.

Ed Cooper, Traverse City Local 2265:

We knew about [unions before 1937], but it took up to that time. You see at that time Detroit was very strong organized labor. Grand Rapids was probably mediocre because they had that Dutch element in there that was always fighting local labor. We took in a lot of members when the airport went in. That's what built the local up. And the Empire Airbase. That was the other big factor. Those were during the war— government jobs. [We organized a union] for the betterment of all carpenters in the area. The carpenters organized to stabilize wages for the same type of work. Everybody was going every which way, all kinds of wages, all kinds of conditions. The boys figured that if we all got together and come up with one answer then we'd all work under the same conditions.

L.M. "Boots" Weir, Detroit Millwrights Local 1102:

I grew interested [in a union] after I became a millwright. My company, Mechanical Handling Systems, had a rate of 60 cents an hour and they missed the job. [Another company] would bid lower and get the job. I'd go over to the other [company] and work for 40 cents, just to be busy. We had no stability whatever. There was no [unemployment insurance]. You had to get out there and get it. It was a sad sight when my company would miss the job when they paid me a buck an hour and I would go down and work for 75 cents [for the company that bid the job cheaper]. I was cutting the throat of the company which really sponsored my training. It was pitiful thing, but you had to be at work. It was quite a cut throat game. My superintendent said to me, "Hey, I could get jobs if you would work that cheap for me." Along with that "Why don't you guys get organized?" In a friendly way. "Why don't you guys get organized so you would all get the same?" This came from my superintendent. There was a lot of advice like that came from management, in order to stabilize the industry. They might get other equipment cheaper, but they wouldn't be able to play with labor like that. This is where the desire came to get organized.

Of course the national emergency had come on the scene preparatory to WW II and we had sought organization in different places throughout the late 1930s—the conveyor workers of this particular area. The Machinists had some shops, the Iron Workers had some shops. Even the C.I.O. Skilled Trades local had some shops, the Millwrights had some shops. Throughout '38, '39, '40 we was in kind of a no-man's land. We were all split up. Conveyor workers as such were in three or four different organizations. The Trades were engaged at Dawson Food Products, the old Pepsi Cola plant on Gratiot Avenue and with the aid of the Teamsters who were able to conduct an effective strike there. The Building Trades moved in and organized their rightful jurisdiction, and the Millwrights got us.

Prior to that I was with a small committee that went to the District Council of Carpenters and talked with the then Secretary-Treasurer Finnley Allen. We told him who we were, what we done, that we felt like millwrights, our individual employers called us millwrights, and how we'd bounced around, and he said, "Well, you finally found the right place." From that we began to concentrate in Local 1102, 1940, '41 that's when this happened. I never belonged to any other union. When we got in here we found all kinds of mechanics, from setting powerhouse equipment, printing equipment, so we all came together that way.

Conveyors were in their infancy at that time, storage and transportation being their main function. From that it went right into automation and it just hasn't reached its end. When I began they didn't necessarily call us apprentices. They called us helpers, or flunkies, or what have you. Finally when we got into a union we established an apprenticeship. I'd go to the meetings and keep spouting off, you know, and from that, they elected me and that just kept growing. Added capacity, added responsibilities. In '52 I sought the District Council and left the Local union. Of course I never came back. I always kept my membership here, and always will. I'll never transfer my membership.

Circumstances might also bring the worker from one International union into another, when jurisdictions shifted to accommodate changes in methods and materials.

David Charlton, Detroit Resilient Floor Local 2265:

The union hadn't started yet. That's where our local originated at Turner Brooks. It started in 1933. We started trying to get organized and then we joined the Upholsterers. We were with them two or three years and then we shifted over to the Painters. We were with them two or three years and from there we shifted over to the Carpenters. We joined them in 1939.

Gerald Gavin, Detroit Resilient Floor Local 2265:

Prior to 1939 there was a controversy throughout the country with the floor covering people as to what International Union they were going to belong to. They call it the Peter Eller decision—I don't know who Peter Eller was but they called it the Peter Eller line which was the Mississippi River. On one side they all went into the Painter's Union and on the other side, which we are on, they all went into the Carpenters' Union.

Michael Belles, Detroit Resilient Floor Local 2265:

I was in the Cement Finishers Union and two of us laying tile with that card and there were two carpenters spreading the cement. The rest of the crew were carpenters from Chicago. That was a union job. I stayed as a cement finisher until 1939 when we were working on the Veterans Hospital in Dearborn and Vern Lowe asked me for my card and I gave it to him and he promptly tore it up and said, "You're a carpenter now. Just keep on working." The first union I joined was the Cement Finishers.

Conditions of work often are their own persuaders. The daily work routine, the interaction with a foreman or other supervisor, and the sounds, sights and smells of the work place mould a person's consciousness. When those conditions are particularly oppressive, one looks for a way to change them.

Wilbur Slye, Escanaba Local 1832:

I went to work in the paper mill [in Gladstone]. They paid me 24 cents an hour and it was seven days a week. We figured that the company was so obnoxious—not the company, I don't think, as much as some individuals. It always seemed to me that if supervision would treat people like human beings, there would be no need for having a union, but they seem to abuse people. So I said what you need in this place is a good union. The Paper Makers at that time were organized. I went to one of the Paper Makers and got some information from him and wrote some letters, and got an organizer, to come to my house, got some of my wife's relations that worked there at that time, and he got some more and the results was that we got the nucleus of a union started. You didn't go out and have a meeting unless you had enough power, so you had these people come to your home first. You didn't want anyone to notice that you was a union man, because then you're an agitator and a trouble maker. It was survival, was all it was. It was just survival. I guess I realized that that was the only way you could survive. The Paper Makers had an organization, and they seemed to get along very good and the company respected those people, and that might have been the reason why [I thought of a union].

Michael Sammon, Detroit Local 337:

There was a few in the union [when I came here from Canada], but as far as the Contractors were concerned, if they saw your card they wouldn't even hire you. [I joined] February 1923. It wasn't [Local] 337. There was another local on the East side. Frank O'Neil was president. There was no District Council then. I had no experience [with unions] whatsoever. I read about it a little bit, but I had it in my mind all along. I figured that was the only way for workers to have control of the jobs.

Victor Weiner, Saginaw Resilient Floor Local 2585:

The neighborhood [I lived in] one time rebelled against the butcher when he started raising prices. They got together in the neighborhood to picket the butcher. This all must have been when I was eleven, twelve years old, [right after WW I]. This taught me what it was to pull together, that you couldn't do anything on your own. That's my first indoctrination about picket lines and what can be done collectively. I worked for Yellow Cab Company and quite a few of our guys got together and we didn't know what union was what. We heard about the Teamsters, and we sent one of our boys to talk to the Teamsters to see if they could do something for us, and at that time the Teamster weren't as big as they are now. They weren't concerned about taxi drivers about 1925, '26. We were on our own. We had to battle the best we could and we all lost our jobs. I didn't know too much about unions at that time. I only knew that collectively we could do more than I could do by myself. The guys stuck together as long as they could, but there was no leadership.

My Uncle was very union-minded, 'cause when he was in New York, he had joined the union. He found out how they were being treated here [in Saginaw], kids making $1.50 a day. Well we were looking for help, but they didn't know the work properly. My Uncle said, "they got to have a union here where they got an apprenticeship school to learn properly." So he got some others and myself and we petitioned the International [Carpenters] for a charter, and they got it. I was in business and I seen the need for it. That was local 2272. Then they busted up and everybody went into local 334. They were in with the carpenters and that business agent wasn't concerned about the floor coverers. Then they got Local 593. I signed up in September 1940 [when] it was chartered. I paid my dues and carried a card. I thought it was an honor. We lasted then until about 1945. Then there was problems among themselves; they wanted to join the Painters, but the Carpenters had the jurisdiction, so we all went back into 334.

After a while, our members were dropping out like mad—floor coverers—[because they weren't getting the attention] from the business agent of 334. I was doing pretty well in my business, but I didn't give a hang which way it went. I made a point that I was going to stick with it, to keep the Local going. I was pretty well fixed at that time that I could make that kind of statement. I had wanted to be in business, I did and I made a success of it, but I told them this time if they wanted to start a union they'd have to stick with it and not be prima donnas. So we sent a kid down [to Indianapolis] and he talked to some people and he said we would hear from them. Two, three months later a man came into my place of business. He was kinda puzzled, why a place of business. He introduced himself as Harry Pulver. I told him who I was. He said, "I understand that some people here want to start a union."

I said, "you're right."

He said he was surprised. I told him that I would see that they stuck with it. I gave him my background and told him that I hadn't forgotten where I come from, so he understood. I had forty people [at the first meeting]. We had quite a meeting. That's when 2585 started.

Ralph Krimmel, Industrial Council, Battle Creek:

[During my apprenticeship] my employer wanted me on the job all the time and not to take the time off to attend the apprenticeship classes. And we had a little go-around over that, but I finally did finish my apprenticeship classes in school as prescribed, which I am glad that I did. That, I think, got me involved with the union because we had at that time several discussions and it got me interested and from that day on I kinda chaired meetings and things for the industrial segment of our shop.

The reasons for joining the United Brotherhood of Carpenters and Joiners, like the reasons for becoming a carpenter, include tradition, circumstances, conditions, lessons learned from the efforts of others. Joining the union had little significance for some. They did it because it was an accepted part of the routine of work. However, when a union began to organize, a worker faced the old union question: Which side are you on? The answer could prove lasting and profound.

Bill Potter, Detroit Resilient Floor Local 2265:

When this local organized they were picketing Crowley's and J.L. Hudson's and we would haul all the merchandise which was sold today to the garage for delivery the next day. We knew just exactly where all the jobs to install the linoleum were. The Steward came over and he said "Look you know where these lay jobs are. How about slipping us the addresses."

I said, "fine, so long as we don't get into trouble." So when someone went out to install the jobs these fellows would be there and run them off. Nobody got wise to it.

But one day the boss came to me and he said, "I can't understand it. Every job that comes out of here to be laid there's a union guy there to run these guys off. We don't know where this comes from."

I said, "I don't know anything about that. I just deliver the stuff."

He said, "If you see where these guys hide their picket signs, go over there and destroy them." I wouldn't do that.

Ed Harper, Berkeley Local 998:

In 1924 I joined the Union, Local 1032, Pontiac. Pontiac was not a union town, but they had that small union there and some of the union members talked to me, working on the job. I was thirty years old and had been working as a carpenter about eight years. When I joined I was converted and like other converts, I was more active than a convert into some religious organization. I spent a couple nights a week talking to brother carpenters trying to get them to join the union. [What converted me was] the idea that organization would help, and it certainly did.

Ezell Johnson, Battle Creek Local 871:

[The journeyman carpenter I worked for] said "The war's going to freeze up all the material." (It had [already] just about frozen. All we could get was rough stuff.) "[The railroad] is calling all the old railroad men back," he said "I lack two years of getting my time in so I can get my pension. I'm going back to the railroad to get my thirty years in. You go down to the Local (Thursday nights we had the meetings). You join the carpenters' local and you stay in there 'cause there's going to be work from now on."

I remember his words as if he were saying them. He said, "Now, if you need me, I can help you ('cause he was in the Local) go down and take the examination."

I said, "I believe I can make it."

He said, "I know you can, but you might get nervous, and I'd like to be there to help you."

I said, "If you're going down there, it's okay. I appreciate it, but I can make it, I'm sure." I had that much confidence in myself. And I missed one question and that was cabinet building. He really insisted on my doing that. That was the beginning of my life, and I just love that man for it. He's dead now, but it seems he still lives on, because he really give me a lift for the rest of my life.

Whether tradition or necessity brought the carpenter into the union, he stayed because it worked. A worker may have entered the union just as he entered the trade, learning from and following his father's example. Contractors may have brought a worker into an apprenticeship program, or insisted that he have a union card, proof that he had passed the test and was a certified journeyman carpenter, qualified to do the work. No doubt the great organizing drives of the 1930s created an atmosphere which legitimized union membership and brought many into the carpenters' ranks. Perhaps the example of others proved decisive, as in the case of Wilbur Slye who saw the respect organized paper makers received, or Vic Weiner who saw his neighbors effectively organize to protest rising meat prices.

For many, objective conditions in the work itself brought them to the conclusion Ed Harper reached: organization "would help." Few saw a revolution in organization. Rather as "Boots" Weir pointed out, it brought stability. It would end cut-throat competition between carpenters and create apprenticeship programs to teach the trade and thus assure higher quality in its practice. As Ed Cooper put it, the union was designed "for the betterment of all carpenters in the area."

Throughout its history, the Brotherhood has struggled to create stability, to protect standards, and to work for the betterment of all carpenters. Carpenters have often debated, sometimes bitterly, how to protect standards, how best to create stability, and how to achieve the betterment of all carpenters. They have also debated, sometimes heatedly, who should be included in "all carpenters," but the goals have never been obscure.

Chapter III
Working With the Tools

Laying floor. That was hard work. Nobody knows how hard it was until you got your back broken in so that you could do that. Guys used to chew tobacco and spit under there and when you lay your's down behind them, that was a dirty deal. And then they'd nail your apron down.

Jake Michel, Saginaw Local 334

Early Years

Craftsman often feel special relationships with their tools and with the materials upon which they use those tools. How complex those relationships may be, will emerge in this chapter. Primarily those relationships express themselves in the work itself, for tools are not gems, worn to adorn, but practical implements used to make a living. One would still find tools used a century ago on the work site today, but many tools have changed, as have methods of using tools. Appropriately, we shall listen to the work experiences of Michigan carpenters in order to understand these relationships and we shall begin with the early years.

Merlin Veysey, Saulte Ste. Marie Local 46:

Nineteen fifteen, sixteen. The winter before, we went up the road and cut one log, just one log of pine. It took us a whole week to saw through it with an eight foot crosscut saw. My brother and I started through. One cut. We got it out of the bush with one sleigh. Rolled it on there with the horses and chained it down, and dragged it home that way. Took it over to the Mill on [highway 29]. And that's where they sawed that up. One log is all we took out of there: five foot across the butt. Pure white pine. The nicest pine, you'll ever see.

My dad and I made all the windows, door frames, and I mean the sash, and everything, for that one house. We built a house ourselves, him and I, the trim and everything. He had a tool box about four feet long, about two feet wide and twenty-some inches high with nothing but wooden planes that would make any kind of design you want for a cornice, for putting the panels in your doors, you could fit them in there just like nothing. By hand. Him and I did that all one winter.

Merlin Vesey, Sault Ste Marie Local 46

Elmer Swanson, Escanaba Local 1832:

We got all our lumber in the rough. I don't know why, but they never attempted to do any carpenter work in the winter time. If my father would line up a home or two for the following spring and summer, we would make the frames for the windows then in our spare time. We had a big long work bench. Everything was done by hand. To make things straight, like for a jamb, you couldn't do that with a short plane. We used a three foot wooden plane. They were about three inches wide. It was quite a trick to use them, too. Sometimes I wish I would have saved them. I had a complete set of them. When we moved from one job to another, we used to have to get a dray, a horse and a wagon, to move our work bench and tool boxes from one job to another.

In them days we laid hardwood floor, usually oak in living rooms and bedrooms and in the kitchen it was maple. We had to scrape them by hand, before varnishing. And that was quite a trick too, because if you made a gouge of any kind, it would show in the finish. You'd usually get right down there on your knees, and there'd be piles of shavings on the floor.

Window frames were quite a job. When you had to make that rabbet for that parting stop that separates your upper sash from the lower, that had to be plowed out by hand. The basement windows were the roughest, because they were made out of two inch planking and we'd have to cut a groove 3/8 inch deep by an inch and 3/8, the thickness of the sash. First we would cut a 3/8 inch rabbet down through at the inch and 3/8 point. We had another little plane that we would take the rest of that out with. I'm telling you, that was really some work. Hard work.

Roman Dunneback, Lansing Local 1449:

The first two years in carpentry you did bull work. The apprentice got saw work, by hand cutting rafters all day and cutting floor joist ends. Anything the senior carpenters on the job wanted cut up, why the apprentices done it. We drilled all our own holes for all the locks and chiseled out all our plates, and everything by hand. [Wages] finally got to 90 cents and $1.00, but you worked for it. And I think you should work for it.

Ray Skiba, Alpena Local 1132:

The old time carpenters didn't seem to want to teach you anything, so all we were doing was putting on sheeting and putting roofs on, nailing hardwood floors. We never got a chance to do any trim work.

I think the first window, or door that I cased was after six years of working at the trade.

It was all bull work for the carpenter helper. Your saw and hammer was just the same as it is today, but you used to sand floors by hand. I remember using wood planes. You had some fancy chisels. Outside of a hammer and saw and a level, trisquare, six foot rule, the contractor furnished most of your tools. You just couldn't afford to buy tools. Some of the antiques I got [from] the tool box that [my dad] had. That was promised to me before he passed away. My mother made sure that I got them before anybody else got their hands on it. He had a great big wooden box that he kept everything in. Of course, he used to use broad axes and everything else. It was just a conglomeration of all kinds of tools. Sometimes you had to peel your own cedar posts, and that was part of the carpenter's work at that time. I [also] have the old original wood tool box, the hand made one that he used to carry on the jobs.

Leonard B. Zimmerman, Grand Rapids Local 335 and General Representative, UBJA.

There was an old Swedish carpenter I worked with—an excellent trim carpenter—he taught me how to take care of my hand tools, how to sharpen them, how to set them down so you didn't set them on the cutting edge. He said, "Have you got a scraper?" A scraper is for taking out indentations for hardwood, scrape it off, rather than plane it.

"No,"

"Well, when you come to work Monday, bring a couple of bucks with you." I'd scrape up two bucks and come to work Monday and he'd have an old two-hand scraper. I remember one time he brought me a Stanley scraper; I still got the thing down the basement. I paid a dollar and a half for it. This old mechanic had gone down to those old used tools stores on South Division Avenue and scrounged around and found this old scraper for a buck and a half. He charged me just exactly what he paid for it.

Those were the old timers that took care of the young guys if you wanted to apply yourself and wanted to learn the trade and were serious about it. They didn't take any back talk, but if you got along with the old timers, they taught you everything they knew. They'd tell you what to do and when to do it. You were a gofer for them. Whatever they'd tell you to do, you'd do it! They were boss!

Getting to the job posed its own problems, particularly when the carpenter owned all his own tools and carried them in the chest he had made as an apprentice.

Jake Michel, Saginaw Local 334:

Them days we moved around from one job to another on a bicycle. You'd put your [hand] box on the handle bars and go from one job to the other. The big box you'd hire twenty-five or fifty cents to have your tool box hauled home. When you were on the next job, the boss would take them around. Once you were done, it seems to me, you had to take care of your own tools.

Time and distance fell to technology for carpenters just as it fell before Americans generally. The automobile brought the carpenter more quickly to his work site, although it did not solve all his transportation problems and may have created for him the most modern problem between father and son.

Elmer Swanson, Escanaba Local 1832:

One job that my dad built was out in the country which is Danforth. That would be nine miles one way. Well, he'd have to walk that or he would get a ride with a farmer. In 1919, I bought a Model T Ford. My dad didn't care to have me buy it at first, but I did anyhow. Then he began to see what a wonderful thing that was, how you could get out to these jobs. Nine miles away, that was nothing, in a Model T. You could go out there and come home the same day. So then Dad says, "I'll pay half of it."

I said, "Oh no you don't. Some night when I want to go out with it you'll say, 'Wait a minute. I own half of that car.' We'll use it for the work, but I'll own it." A tool box in them days was as big as that [coffee] table only higher. I had two of them. We had huge tool boxes, but in later years, we had like a suitcase. With the Model T we could haul a lot of tools, but the big tool boxes we had then, I don't think we could even put it in the Model T.

The huge tool chests gave way to smaller, lighter boxes as the tools themselves evolved. The technology which built the automobile influenced the design of carpenters' tools as well.

Ed Cooper, Traverse City Local 1461:

The Stanley, Sergeant and Bailey were the primary ones that made [iron] planes and they all come out in just about the same time. There was a smoothing plane, a scrub plane, a block plane and a little trimming plane. There was an enormous amount of planes, rabbeting planes, and skew planes, and everything. When you got into these [with interchangeable blades] you eliminated carrying so many of the other wood block planes.

Ed Cooper, Traverse City Local 1461

Stanley came out with what they called 32, 35, 45 and 55 planes. There was quite a few changes added to all metal planes to compensate for the need of not carrying so many planes. From 1891 right up to 1920 they made changes in the planes. The only place you would find mostly where they are using them [now] is in some museum where they have an old fellow in there that is using the tools just to show people what they were used for. Just like a car, the models change; as you go along you discard the ones, and hang on to the better ones that's coming out.

The old square had an 18" tongue and a 24" blade. The newer ones were all set standard with a 16" tongue and 24" blade. The rafter table was on the square: six inch rise, eight inch rise, twelve inch rise, all the way up to twenty-four inch rise. That's all right on the square. You set your bevel on the scale and you can actually measure from the bird's mouth—that's the cut that sets on the plate—right up to the peak. It's all on the square, so that simplifies it. Actually the square today, the carpenter won't take it out of the box but once a week using it. The fellow that I worked with he could set down and pretty near read the Bible off the square. He said, "There's nothing in the world that you can't answer on the steel square. Any mathematical problem of any kind, it's on the steel square." He was master of the square, as far as I was concerned.

The skew back saw looks more like an item that you'd like to have in preference to the straight back. It dresses the saw up a little bit. Everybody carries a hammer, but most of them now don't carry a wood handled hammer. The older carpenters still stand by them. They like the wood handle because there is an action in the handle itself. You don't get a recoil in the wrist. Driving heavy nails all day with a bad hammer, you got to have somebody pick up your hand and put it in you pocket to take it home with you. The older carpenters used to thin the handle up in the throat and that limbered it up enough so that it took the recoil off from traveling up into your arm, but it also let the head of the hammer hang onto the nail, instead of bounding back off the nail. We used to take linseed oil and rub the handle with several coats and that penetrated and kept the handle [from] drying out and being brittle. It was always an active handle. Carpenters used to carry from a 13 ounce up to a 28 ounce hammer. The 28 ounce was for framing, for heavy work. I didn't care much for them. I figured I could do as much with a 16 or 18 ounce hammer. Standard carpenter's hammer is a 16 ounce hammer.

Cornelius Vos, Muskegon Local 100:

You usually carried a pretty good sized hatchet and you carried three saws: one coarse saw, one really fine toothed saw, and big rip saw. And you always had chisels with a mallet of some description. I've got a [tool box] downstairs yet that is quite fancy. We always had a brace and bit, planes. I always had a saw set and files [to set the teeth]. A saw has got teeth. [Each is canted out]. You had to learn to sharpen [and set] saws. That was part of your trade. I do all my own filing. A saw wouldn't work without it being set.

This little Frenchman had an antique outfit that he would [place on the blade] of the saw and hit that with a hammer. That would push the teeth out. He could put a needle [between the rows of teeth] and it would run right straight down, from the top to the bottom. He was a little saw filer from the sawmills. I saw it done.

You had to cut [lumber] the right length. You bought eight foot, ten foot, twelve, fourteen, sixteen foot two by fours and some of them wasn't even cut the right length. You couldn't put them on until you cut them.

Elmer Swanson, Escanaba Local 1832:

I remember the first iron plane I bought at Delta Hardware here in Escanaba. My dad fixed up my credit there and I went down and bought a thirty-six inch iron plane. Today there isn't a carpenter who would carry a thing like that. That thirty-six inch iron plane weighed half as much as some of the carpenters' tool boxes. That took the place of that big long wooden one. Oh, it was nice. It cut nice and it handled nice, and everything about it.

Jake Michel, Saginaw Local 334:

My dad told me that if he was ever done with them, those tools were mine, and I prized them as much as he did. He made an oval top on his [box]. I wondered why they did that. They tell me that when you used to come from the old country, all the trunks were oval top. The reason for that is that they used to lash the trunks on the deck. The water wouldn't lay on the trunk and seep into it. The water would roll off. When I started out he gave me a little hand box. I had my saw and level and wrecking bar, rule: things necessary to start out with. I still have the first saw. My dad bought it for me when I first started. I've got the level and the hand axe. I think the old hammer is gone. And I got the plane he got me when I first started. A little joiner.

He was working on some store fixtures and at noon there was a small fire in the place. Four of them were working on the second or third floor and they went up to pick up their tools because they figured that maybe they wouldn't be working that afternoon on account of the

Saves 5 Men's Labor . . .

And then the Nason Construction Co., Swampscott, Mass., follow this up by saying:

"We cut sills, joists, studding, braces, frames, rout studs for belt, make Jack rafter cuts, all angle cuts of various degrees, rout for stair risers and treads, make window frames, use the machine in cutting flooring, trim and in fact from the commencement of the construction to its completion.

"We figure that we save 5 men's labor by using the DeWalt Wonder Worker and advance the completion of our job fully 25% sooner than we could without it."

DeWalt Wonder Worker

fire. Coming down the elevator the paint room exploded and caught the four of them in the elevator. The four of them were killed in the elevator. 1924.

The Application of Power

One of the most dramatic changes in the daily work routine of the carpenter came about through the application of powered saws on the work site. The first buzz saws were large and cumbersome, not at all like the hand held saws made possible by the development of small electric motors.

Jake Michel, Saginaw Local 334:

We only had big one lunger [saws]. You had a table, and a gasoline engine was sitting way beyond them. We used to rip things on them. Cut-off was always done by hand, but the ripping before we got the Dewalt saws, was done by these gasoline engine saws. The first one we got showed up about the early 1920s.

Ed Cooper, Traverse City Local 1461:

When we worked at the airport, I run a saw continually. 1942 I run a big Novo four cylinder gasoline engine saw. It had a kick feed, where the saw travels back and forth a ways on the top. Your saw travels about sixteen, eighteen inches back and forth on a roller, the whole saw. You had a kick feed on the bottom. It was the same principle [as the radial arm saw] but that saw travels overhead and this travelled on the table. Instead of using my hand [to pull it], there was a foot treadle. It had a sixteen inch blade. It was out in a field where you didn't have to run a bunch of cords to it. You just gassed her up and it would run all day on a tank of gas.

A lot of that [power equipment] didn't come in until they started putting temporary electrical service in on the project. When we first started out they never even thought of anything like that. They started that in '45, '50 for house construction. On industrial sites they had service before that.

Ezell Johnson, Battle Creek Local 871:

There was very little ripping done after '43 with a hand saw. They had power table saws.

Electrical power on the job site, whether from portable generators or a temporary service, transformed sawing from a dull, tedious and exhausting job to a task quickly and easily performed. The first saws

brought with them their own share of problems, ranging from safety to efficiency.

Walter Weir, Mt. Clemens Local 674:

[In 1939] Skil made the old Sears Craftsman; I call it the old alligator, with the gear box, not the straight drive. The one with the gear box. They was all heavy when they first come out.

Grady Pinner, Berkeley Local 998:

I first got into power saws about 1945. Up until that time they were few and far between. The earlier ones were not much better than hand saws, they were so heavy and so clumsy. You had to warm them up, they wouldn't run. They had grease and the grease would get stiff.

About everything you can do nowadays with power, except think.

Vincent Kowalski, Mt. Clemens Local 674:

I was working out at Romulus when them [Skill saws come in]. They put us all out there on a Saturday for overtime. They got an electrician to run a line, and they took two or three saws off that one line. The guy out on the end started sawing and the guys in the middle wouldn't have [power]. You could watch the teeth go around.

[Dangerous?] Carpenters are pretty level headed people. There was some of them careless, especially when they got into rushing things, but I don't think it was dangerous. I think the worst danger was scaffoldings.

Grady Pinner, Berkeley Local 998:

The craft is reasonable safe now. You can get chewed up by the power saw, if you are not careful. The carpenters have learned to respect the power tools more than they used to. Some of it is we have better working conditions out there.

Regrets over the passing of older hand tools do not disturb the carpenter at work. Few romantic yearnings for the "good old tools" overpower practical considerations.

Elmer Swanson, Escanaba Local 1832:

[I had no regrets about replacing those wooden planes.] God, no! It was easier.

We used to stand there and cut rafters by hand. Holy man: the days we cut by hand, you'd be surprised how fast we worked. We kept our saws very sharp.

Michael Sammon, Detroit Local 337:

I built two or three tool boxes. I gave them away. You didn't need something that big. You'd just take a hand box with a few things, what you really needed.

Them days are all gone by. It was all right, it was fine, working with the guys. I don't see any difference in the tools.

Roman Dunneback, Lansing Local 1449:

[My dad's] tool box was sold to my sisters. When he passed away there was six of us brothers still living. There would have been a little fight there if one of us would have said "It's mine." I did not want it.

I've give away a lot of old antiques [tools], because I'm not for 'em. We live with what we got today, what's handed to us today. I wouldn't want to go back.

Merlin Veysey, Sault Ste. Marie Local 46:

I'll tell you the truth about it. This is no lie. Two years ago I sold all my tools. You know what I sold? I'll tell you what I sold. I sold them nothing. It's just junk. If I was to carry that tool box in on a job today, they'd laugh me right off it. Everything I had in there you had to use by hand. Today you carry a Skil saw and a drill. Today everything is electric.

Ed Cooper, Traverse City Local 1461:

My main reason for collecting tools, I restore them, and put them back in condition so somebody in the next hundred years will still see them.

The Romance of Wood

There is something fresh and crisp and clean about the smell of new lumber. Carpenters often mention that, but the most important qualities of wood arise from its creative potential: what can it become?

Ray Skiba, Alpena Local 1132:

There are things you can do with wood that you can't do with metal, steel, or anything else. You got different kinds of wood to work with. Of course you got your sugar pine. It's clear. Of course it is pretty near out of reach as far as expense today. There isn't a knot in it and you can get it two inches thick. I've worked with that stuff. It's real nice to handle.

Aloe's "Jiffy" Saw

Ed Cooper, Traverse City Local 1461:

Most of the older houses around Traverse City are framed up with hemlock. It was the best wood available at that time. It came out of big stock and didn't have a lot of knots in it.

Now, your two by fours are only an inch and a half by three and a half. We used to get them three and five-eighths by one and five eighths. The even measurements [simplify], but in strength it cuts down. Probably out of a fair sized log you'd probably pick up five or six more two by fours than what you did before.

At one time they had some big timber in this area, and they needed a long saw. That was cork pine. It's real soft. It's in the white pine family. It was one of the better logs, because there were very few knots in it, it was pretty much all clear. That was back when they were cutting the big stuff and burning the stuff that had a knot in it.

Cornelius Vos, Muskegon Local 100:

I have a hundred different kinds of wood carved into [Herons]. From the time that I was a kid, I have always liked wood. I have a couple logs from a Michigan white pine twenty inches across, split up drying in my garage.

I'll carve little men or something. You can't buy Michigan white pine, hardly. It's the nicest wood to work there is.

It would be possible to replicate the experience of working with the hand tools used commonly in building during the early decades of this century. Those tools are largely still available at a well-stocked hardware store or lumber yard. The tools have not really been lost, except, perhaps, the wood block planes which one would find in the holdings of tool collectors like Ed Cooper. And we could find old timers like the Swedish carpenter who took Len Zimmerman under his wing, who could train us to use those tools. From the perspective of a working carpenter, however, that would be simply romantic nonsense. He would agree with Roman Dunneback that "we live with what we got today."

Tools have evolved. The wood block planes gave way to metal planes with interchangeable blades. They in turn gave way to industrial processes which made molding quicker and cheaper. In the old days, a carpenter started in the hole and handed over the key to the owner. Everything was made on the job site or in the individual carpenter's shop. Today, the job site is largely the place of assembly of parts and components manufactured elsewhere. That is the modern way and however much he may regret the passing of the old ways, the carpenter would not return to them. Not all carpenters would agree with Red Vesey that the old tools he sold were junk, but they would be no more willing to make their living working with them, than they would be willing to abandon their pick-up trucks for the bicycles carpenters used to ride to work. That would simply be absurd.

Some things remain constant through this change, however, no carpenter would be without a hammer, and to every construction carpenter, there is something special about working outdoors amid the smell of sawdust and new wood.

Chapter IV
Flooring, Factory and Pile Driving

One of our guys was still an apprentice, but he wanted to become a journeyman.
He told Norm, "I'm good enough to become a journeyman. Why don't you write the
committee to make me a journeyman?"

Norm sent him out on a job to do a bathroom. So he goes out to the job and puts
the tile down and does a beautiful job around the tub and the toilet. It's all done and
the journeyman goes in to check the job, picks up the toilet and moves it over. It wasn't
where it was supposed to be.

Gerald Gavin, Local 2265

Not all members of the United Brotherhood of Carpenters and Joiners
work intimately with wood. New processes and new materials have altered
the trade, but they have not altered the pride of craftsmanship. Hardwood
flooring has almost disappeared from the construction business.[1] Factories
which specialized in manufacturing it, like Bruce Hardwood Flooring
Mill where Ezell Johnson got his first job, are today rare. Working amid
piles of shavings, planing the floors by hand, the carpenter cursed the
slow and tedious process. As Ray Skiba put it. "I would hate to wish
on anybody to sand a hardwood floor by hand. My God! That was work."

Today sub-floors and floors are laid in sheets of plywood, particle
board or other new materials, eliminating hours of backbreaking work.
Such a change occurred not only because of new materials, but because
of a shift in taste toward carpeting and tile.

Gerald Gavin, Detroit Resilient Floor Local 2265:
When our carpet industry started to boom, the hardwood floor
industry went to hell. They put that cheap plywood in.

David Charlton, Detroit Local 2265:
There's two phases to this trade. The majority of them were in the
hard surface business, that's linoleum and asphalt tile. Then there was
the carpet end of it, which I was in practically all my life.

When I first came here I don't believe there were over twelve carpet
layers in the city of Detroit. They were all old men. When I first started
the carpet was twenty-seven inches, most of it, and these women would
sew it into a 9 x 12, or a 12 x 20, needle and a thread.

Gerald Gavin, Michael Belles, Bill Potter, David Charlton, Tom Suarez, Detroit Resilient Floor Local 2265

Gerald Gavin, Local 2265:

Back then all your good carpets were made in 27 inch widths, and the reason being was, if the center part wore out you didn't have to replace the whole thing. Then they came out with the broadloom which was 9 foot carpet and 12 foot and then 15 foot which did nothing but create productivity because it's a helluva lot easier to go out and install a job if you don't have any sewing to do.

Vic Weiner, Saginaw Resilient Floor Local 2585:

Floor covering is part of the carpenters' trade. A lot of people don't realize that floor covering is a trade. They think it is a specialty. There's lots of work we used to do in floor covering, with carpeting, with linoleum. We could do a lot of that work, sewing things in, we could make emblems and all that stuff. On the floor we could put compasses or a company's trade mark. Nowadays they have that manufactured.

We used to spit tacks. With a tack hammer, hammer them in. The tackless strip came in about '43.

The tools have remained fairly much the same. There was a time when we didn't have the stretcher to stretch the carpet tight.

David Charlton, Detroit Resilient floor Local 2265:

I, more than once, went on Inter-Urbans. You'd get on down here on State and Woodward—Crowley's was just a block away—and go to Flint on that Inter-Urban. You'd go up through fields and you'd be rocking up and down and swaying. It was quite an experience.

Michael Belles, Detroit Local 2265:

The guys who were laying tile had to get on with their gas can, and their torches, and the conductors would [tell them to] get the hell off.

David Charlton, Detroit Resilient Floor Local 2265:

You had to carry a roller, which weighed about 100 pounds, your torch, squares, and some guys carried three tool boxes full of paint and coloring—and all kinds of putty.

That old Battleship linoleum has been on the floor in the Edwin Denby building since 1930 when it was built. It was heavy.

Bill Potter, Local 2265:

I knew a guy by the name of McCandless out here in Pontiac who could cut a seam in one stroke right through that goddamn stuff [battleship linoleum]. I couldn't believe it. I looked, and I said "are you cutting that with one cut?"

He said, "Yeah."

I said, "Holy Toledo, It takes me three to go through that stuff!"

David Charlton, Local 2265:

At that time everything was made of 100% wool and the best grade of jute available. And now it's made out of paper, and all sorts of fillers to make up the bulk and it's all glues and rubber, heavier than can be.

Gerald Gavin, Local 2265:

I started carpet work in 1948 and I can recall then the tackless strip was just coming out. We used to have to explain to the customer [that] it's just like a curtain stretcher. Prior to that we used to tack the jobs in. The carpet industry started booming when people got away from nine by twelve rugs, and got tired of waxing the perimeter of the floor.

When you went out and installed carpeting with padding, you tacked, you used carpet tacks, all around the outer edges and then you put your shoe molding back to cover up the tacks. Then Roberts came out with a strip of wood about an inch wide and its got pins coming out of it on an angle. You nailed this strip all the way around the outer edge of the room. You hooked the carpet on one end. The pins were on an angle which hooked it. And you stretched it across, hooked on the other pins which were on an angle and you had a beautiful finish. You had a smooth edge. You could never see any tack marks or nothing.

This made a beautiful job, plus cut the installation time down unbelievably. You know, to go along there and spit these tacks was time consuming. You had to make sure you got them under the molding, and so forth. That increased the amount of yards installed from fifty to seventy five, just that one item.

They used to bind around doors and fireplaces, hand sew a binding around. They came out with a soft metal [strip]. Tuck the carpet underneath, hammer it down and you had a beautiful finish. It cut your time again. You're up to 100 yards a day. Everything they have come out with increases the production on the job. It went from a custom job to how much can you do in a day.

If I worked with Dave thirty years ago, and we went out and put in fifty yards of carpet, that was a day's work. Today you go out and put in fifty yards of carpet, it's ten o'clock and you got six more hours to go.

Tile was always nine by nine. All of sudden it was twelve by twelve.

Vic Weiner, Saginaw Local 2585:

The employers we've got today, they don't give a hang. They just want these guys to go out and lay all the carpet they can. The employer treats everyone like he can do the job the same as the next guy. This is a problem. [We believe in] a fair day's work for a fair day's pay.

Bill Potter, Detroit Local 2265:

I think people years ago took pride in their work. I don't think they're doing it today. They don't have time to. The employer is pushing them too hard and the guys just can't do it. Otherwise they can't make a living.

Michael Belles, Detroit Local 2265:

I was laying tile in a long, one story part of a school. There were doors here and there. This carpenter is an old time carpenter, and he's chamfering it, and taking his time and doing a good job. The [contractor] came in and said, "you're costing me a bundle. I expected that you should hang thirty doors a day."

He says "okay, if that's what you want."

The next day at eight o'clock, he gets big spikes and spikes those thirty doors right to the door frame. "There's your thirty doors hung." They call it progress, but all around there's wreckage.

They want to know how fast you are today. And how young you are too. Don't tell them your age when you're asking for a job.

The wood block planes of the early nineteenth century which the carpenter used to make moldings and special cuts for trim gave way to metal planes with interchangeable blades in the later nineteenth century. Even as they were introduced, production of moldings and special trim moved off the work site entirely and into the factory where machines speeded production. Sashes and doors, similarly, were produced in factories far from the actual building site. The carpenter was relieved of a tedious, time-consuming process. He was able to construct and finish his work much more rapidly. Reluctantly, the United Brotherhood of Carpenters and Joiners followed some of that work into the factories and organized semi-skilled workers there. Fitting these workers conceptually into a matrix of craftsmanship has proven difficult for the Brotherhood. Traditionally, the Brotherhood has been committed to organizing around the craft nexus, believing that semi-skilled workers are difficult to organize, that they lack cohesiveness and a common bond. In recent times, the Brotherhood has been more aggressive in organizing such workers, for they understand what it means to defend their interests and protect work standards. Factory work underwent its own changes.

The transformation in tools on the job site had its counterpart in the shop.

Ralph Krimmel, Industrial Council, Battle Creek:

[The introduction of electricity has had a greater impact in the factory] than out on the construction site. You didn't get too mechanized out on the construction site until you did get a portable electric motor. We had the old lineshaft woodworking machinery where maybe as high as twenty machines run off of one line shaft. It run a lathe, a big belt sander, a mortise and a tenon when I first went there. I know I used to run the lathe off of that thing, and believe me it was a hard machine to hold.

A big line shaft, you get vibrations that you don't get off these new [electric] motor driven. Some of those belts used to give somebody a good slap when they come loose.

More significant than the introduction of new tools, however, was the application of the industrial method to the construction of an entire house. Not only were components manufactured far from the construction site, but the house itself.

Ralph Krimmel, Industrial Council, Battle Creek:

[Modular housing] began to develop on the various military bases. This was after the Second World War that I became involved. The Quonset hut and such things were really precut things that were assembled on the job site. This Modular then came along. They set up a factory in Grand Rapids, Michigan, and at that site they constructed and built housing to move onto these sites. They did it in such a way that the thing folded so the thing could be transported down the highway within the limits of the law. It was quite a concept, this house factory. These houses would be transported down the road. The foundation would be prepared and they would be unfolded. There was some work to be done to complete these things on the site. They had to be erected. It wasn't a three pronged plug.

The modular housing industry has achieved neither the popularity nor success its backers sought, but in the long run, its days may be far from over. In the short run, some plants dropped out of production or shifted to other work.

Ralph Krimmel, Industrial Council, Battle Creek

Ralph Krimmel, Industrial Council, Battle Creek:
The Freuhauf plant that this local union represents was involved in the modular industry at one time. [In] the subsequent [shift] to trailer part manufacturing and assembly work, we represented the people and we continue to represent them; we had them when they were modular and we've got them yet.

Chris Craft is one of the manufacturers of boats. This pleasure boat building as you know it today is done with fiberglass, which is a substitute product for our wood. Years ago, Chris Craft products were built almost entirely of wood. The hulls were made of wood and this was all screwed together. This was quite a craft industry. Today the hulls have turned into fiberglass molds. All have to be constructed, formed and shaped with very similar tools and operations to what used to be done with wood. There are still people working at the Chris Craft factory that were working there during the Second World War.

Predominantly [we represent] the man who works with wood and formicas. Our line was woodwork, many years ago, but many, many substances have replaced woodwork over the years, and we claim this jurisdiction. A lot of the plastic substances go along with it. For example, Westinghouse in Grand Rapids, they manufacture moveable office furniture. We once did it, and just because the substance now changes; our work skills are still there and are still involved.

Pile drivers, sometimes known fondly as dock wallopers, have long been members of the Brotherhood and more than any others, carry on the tradition of itineracy, for they frequently travel from site to site, clearing into one local for the duration of a job, but retaining their card in their home local.

Donald McLeod, Sault Ste. Marie Local 46:
I left [Toledo] April 19, 1942, and I was working here on the 21st. They were just starting the MacArthur Lock. The walls on that lock was all wood. [It was] built in 1855.

We drove steel piling and I went out of that right into the carpentry work. We were there fourteen months until that job was done, setting forms, stripping forms, pouring concrete. Then they got a contract to build the southwest pier which was 2100 feet long between the river and the water power canal. They used to have a lot of problems with these old steamers coming in. The suction of the water going into the power plant would tend to suck those boats over there. That took about two years. I was the last man on the job, me and the paymaster.

A job opened up in Sandusky, and a couple of guys from the Soo here went down there. One of them was Campbell R. Moore. We were great friends, and he called me. He said, "this job is going to last all

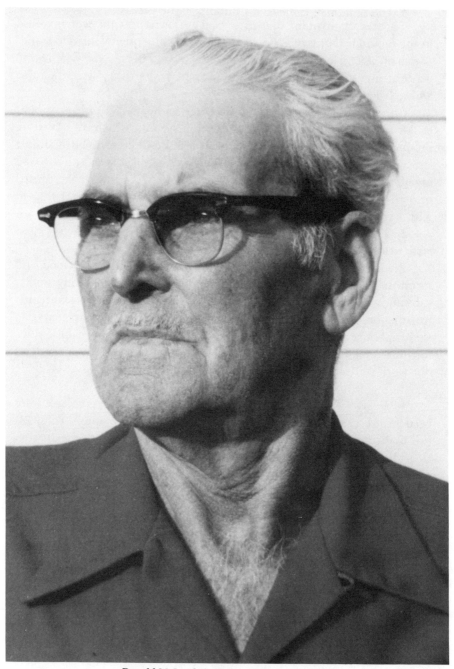

Donald McLeod, Sault Ste Marie Local 46

summer long and it's a good one." I got a job on a little floating derrick, a wooden scow with a truck crane mounted on it.

We were rebuilding the New York Central bridge on Sandusky Bay. The trains used to sneak across it at 8 miles per hour. That was the speed limit, it was in such rough shape. That was on the main line between Cleveland and Chicago. So we started rebuilding that and we never held up the trains. Never held up the trains. When the foundation was in, the track was picked up, new track was already laid, and never stopped the trains.

You put either a wood pile or a steel beam and drive it down into the ground until it can't go any further. That's it. We drove [concrete piling in Toledo] with a Vulcan Hammer. You don't see too many of them now. It's a great big, huge thing. I was the front-end man and made sure it was hanging straight, plumb in all directions, and when you get it all ready to go, you put the hammer on top. When you cut that hammer loose that pile would go just about half its length, and from there on you'd drive it.

I like the steam driven hammers. The only thing is, they are dirty. You have oilers that throw oil in there and you get the steam and the oil together, and you can just imagine.

That big Vulcan, she was very slow. Chunk! Chunk! Nowadays, these hammers just hammer the devil out of those things. They've got these big diesel hammers now that come out of Germany. They burn kerosene. The first one I saw was on the Poe Lock. It was a huge thing. I think it weighed about seven ton. I was afraid to use it at first, they are so big and massive. There are no spark plugs, or nothing, but when you get that hammer on the pile!

Our function at that time [on the Mackinac pipeline job], was digging a trench out in the Straits of Mackinac. On the north side of the straits below St. Ignace, was two big beacons on the shore. One was red and one was green. They were situated so that when you were out on the water one was just a little higher than the other. I stood on the front of the derrick, in line with the crane and watched that set of beacons to see that we didn't get off one way or another.

Out there in the Straits of Mackinac, the terrain under water is practically the same as it is on shore. You get hills and valleys, humps and hollows, rocks and I don't know what all are done there. We had to dig out the high spots and fill in the low spots so this pipe would have a good bed to lay on. It was buried quite a ways out from shore.

The Mackinaw pipeline job developed into a job constructing the most famous structure in Michigan: The Mackinac Bridge. It stands on foundations built by members of the United Brotherhood of Carpenters and Joiners.

Donald McLeod, Sault Ste. Marie Local 46:

I was what they called a working foreman; I worked right along with the men, always.

Merritt, Chapman & Scott kept two of the derricks we used on the pipeline stationed in St. Ignace all winter. In the spring, before we started on the Bridge job, they called myself, and Campbell Moore, and Ed Lowens, and Joe Thwarten.

Everybody that was called back was a foreman, and I was one of them. They were getting all new derricks sent in here. There was a little bit of rivalry between this Ed Lowens and myself. He lived about a mile from here. When the first one came in, we drew straws, who was going to get that derrick. Lowens got the derrick.

The next one came in was the Cherokee. All their derricks was named Indian names. That machine would pick up two hundred twenty-five tons. The big block we called "The Old Man." Eight part line. That is huge, and a big hook. The other line was a whip line. That's got a headache ball on it. You could pick up twenty, thirty ton with a whip line, if you wanted to, but its not good policy.

Merritt, Chapman & Scott decided they would do their own surveying. The Cherokee went out there and probed from the Mackinaw City side straight across on the location of each one of these piers. We had this big huge probe made. It was two hundred and some odd feet long, out of a six inch pipe, with about a three inch hole in the center for air. It was made in two sections. One was a long section with right and left hand threads on it and the other was a short section.

Right in close to shore we could use the short one. But we used the long one most of the time. We would get into position and put the anchors out. That probe was 256 feet long, I believe, and I saw it go out of sight, and we marked on the cable at the water's edge. Due to the exploration we did there, they moved everything north twenty feet.

We built a platform out on the concrete pier which had been filled with rock and poured with concrete, about forty feet in the air. It was built so that this crane could work all the way around. It could travel from one end to the other. I put that up there. Forty feet in the air! The guy that run that crane would have to go up this ladder to get to it. The first morning that he come there to climb up that ladder, he quit: too high in the air for him. This crane handled everything as it come up [to build the pier]. This thing finally ended up way down

Setting the Crane, Mackinaw Bridge construction

in a hole. This was a cable anchorage. We built right around it. I took that [crane] out of there too.

One day my derrick was in the yards. They had the cables up. They had like a cyclone fence that came in huge rolls and every so far it had a cross piece. This particular day there were three iron workers on this tower. They had some sort of pulling apparatus up there. They were pulling this [cyclone fence] up [under the cables]. This was to work off of. You could walk right up it. They put uprights on it and a safety cable, like a rail.

Something happened. Something broke and the thing started to slide back down. One guy was an Indian, full blooded, I think he had one finger and a thumb on one hand, big belt full of wrenches. Two of them men got yanked off of that tower and went overboard. This Indian, he made a leap and he grabbed that wire. He got both hands in that wire and he hung on. That thing slipped way back about half way down. And there he hung. He let go with one hand and he unlaced his boots and his belt and he kicked his shoes off and dropped his belt in the lake and he hung on there until he was rescued. He got his toes in the wire below him. The man was back to work the next day. These other two guys they never found. He was a tough nut, that guy.

The cables were spun down inside those openings on either side, and there are great big hooks down there that the cable goes around. After [the spinning] was all down, the whole thing was filled with concrete. We put all of the piers in. The towers too.

Pile driving was a clear part of the Brotherhoods' jurisdiction a century ago and it remains so today. Despite modest changes in materials: piles are now made of concrete and steel, the job remains virtually the same. The machines which drive the piles have changed in size and speed, but not in purpose or method.

In contrast, the skills and materials used in flooring changed dramatically scarcely a generation ago when taste and technology changed and hardwood flooring yielded to carpet and tile. The Brotherhood, often reluctantly, adapted and followed the work into these new areas and brought within the fold craftsmen who practiced that trade.

New industrial methods forced the Brotherhood into another adaptation. When work was taken off the job site and performed in factories through machine production, the Brotherhood became concerned. This industrial process began in the nineteenth century and its consequences were understood even in 1881, although the Brotherhood struggled internally over the policy of following the work into the factory and organizing those who performed it. Primarily they strove to improve quality and sustain standards by asserting the superiority of the craftsman's product, built on the construction site. Factory production, they argued, resulted in shoddy goods that would embarrass the true craftsman. Within the last score of years the Brotherhood has organized such factories, but the degree of enthusiasm with which this policy has been pursued has varied, frequently generating heated debate. The Industrial Council recognizes both the need to pursue the policy energetically and the distinctive nature of industrial workers' concerns.

Note

[1]Production fell steadily from a high of 1.22 billion board feet in 1955 to 104 million board feet in 1978. *22nd Biennial Edition, Business Statistics*, U.S. Dept. of Commerce, Oct., 1980, 133.

Chapter V
Power Tools and The Carpenter

When I started I didn't see anything but the white [overalls]. In later years they started making these with the stripe. Make you look like you just got out of jail. You don't see white ones anymore, hardly. Mostly you'd see the striped ones. Looks like convicts.

Ezell Johnson, Local 871

The introduction of power tools posed questions about quality and craftsmanship, but it also posed questions about speed ups on the job. Was quantity to become more important to the contractor than quality? We have seen where that could and did happen. When the radial arm saw was introduced it was frequently advertised for its ability to produce. The ads asserted that "One man can do the work of ten." However hyperbolic the claim, it did threaten a central goal of the craftsman: to control the pace and thus the quality of his work. How could he avoid debasement of the craft? It also threatened to displace carpenters, for if one man could do the work of ten, what would happen to the other nine? And who should benefit from the use of these power tools and new methods?

Despite these concerns, carpenters did not oppose the introduction of machinery on the job. The motivation to use power tools is succinctly put by Merlin Veysey: "You use the new [power tools] because they are much easier. Doesn't hurt you so much."

Wilbur Slye, Escanaba Local 1832:

Every worker that I've ever known, is always trying to take a shortcut to improve on a job, or make something simpler. And yet the company gets the benefit. A worker will go and even if he eliminates two or three of his fellow men working alongside of him he goes ahead and says, hey, you can do it this way and eliminate those two guys. That must be human nature.

Ezell Johnson, Battle Creek Local 871:

When you know a trade, you're supposed to know it well enough [that] you should be able to satisfy the contractor. If you can satisfy him, you should be able to satisfy yourself and other people. When you're building houses the contractor got the job, but who done the work? You're building the house. The only thing he done is the figuring. You're the one that actually done the work. When the thing is put together, you're the one who actually put it together. The contractor ain't putting it together. They are just furnishing the money. Now, as I told guys many many times, if you can make a contractor money and you can't make yourself some money, something's wrong. If you can't satisfy yourself and other people by working, there's something wrong.

L.M. "Boots" Weir, Detroit Local 1102 Millwrights:

One thing we never done in the Brotherhood is fight the use of power. The power saw come in, taking them away from the hand saw. The company had to furnish them. Everything is power. We never fought that. Historically it proved [itself]. The membership grew with it. More people became employed.

Some trades have fought the introduction of modern methods. It never was done in our union, and I don't think it has been a detriment. It took an awful rough burden off the man. I can remember we used to climb a ladder with two men and a twenty-four foot length of four inch "I" beam, one on one end, the other on the other. We'd go up that ladder without any rigging or anything, carrying that on our shoulder and putting it into position. That's gone.

I remember when the carpenters fought the use of a chain fall, a chain hand hoist, as a job killer. Well, it really is a man killer not to use them. They get it done faster and its easier on the body of a human being to do it, and more people became employed by it, because the demand got greater. The cheaper you could produce something out there, the greater became your market. But the union did fight the use of power whenever it created an unfair advantage for one carpenter over another.

Carpenters do compete on the basis of their skills, and in the value system of carpenters such competition is not only acceptable, it is welcome. The craftsman who can demonstrate on the job that he can do the work better and more efficiently stakes a claim to that job that other carpenters respect. However, competition based on an individual's ability to buy expensive tools is unacceptable.

Jake Michel, Saginaw Local 334:

There never has been resistance [to power tools]. The only resistance has been to some guys who furnish their own which isn't fair for the other guys.

Anything I can do with power, I'll do.

Vincent Kowalski, Mt. Clemens Local 764:

Years ago they wasn't in so much of a hurry, now, it's production. They wanted quality years ago. They're not so particular now. They want quantity.

When I first started, everything was done by hand. There was no power on the job whatsoever. But it wasn't long before the contractor would have a cut-off saw, or something like that. And then finally they got Skil saws and all kinds of electrical drills and things.

Sylvester "Wes" Helner, Mt. Clemens Local 674:

We had the power saws in the '40s, but there was lots of jobs where you couldn't use them. The Local or the Carpenters' Union wouldn't allow a man to use them unless the contractor furnished it.

Walter Weir, Mt. Clemens Local 674:

The reason for the contractor furnishing power tools, was simple. Wes would come in with a power saw and I wouldn't have any, he'd get the job. I'd be walking down the road talking to myself. That's why it was in the contract that the contractor furnish the power tools. The carpenter furnishes his hand tools. If a [carpenter] can afford to buy all these tools, that gives him a chance to keep the job and the others would be walking down the road.

Sylvester "Wes" Helner, Mt. Clemens Local 674:

A carpenter who had a fair sized family, he couldn't afford to buy all those tools, but a carpenter where it was just him and his wife, he could afford to buy those tools easy, and he could go on the job, and the contractor would say, "Oh, you've got a skill saw? You've got a job."

The fellow that couldn't afford it, they'd lay him off.

Ed Cooper, Traverse City Local 1461:

I've always said that if you wanted power equipment of your own, that's your own prerogative, I wouldn't be without it, but as far as hauling it on the job, I've done that too, but the contractor always paid for my tools. If he wanted to rent them, like he had too many jobs going and he didn't want to invest in more power equipment, he might say, "Why don't you bring yours in and I'll just rent it from you for awhile until we get caught up again. I've done that. They'd set it up on an hourly basis, so much per machine. But then you had the other thing to look at. Some guys would say, "he's letting the contractor get away with this and that." You had to be a little bit cautious on that. One

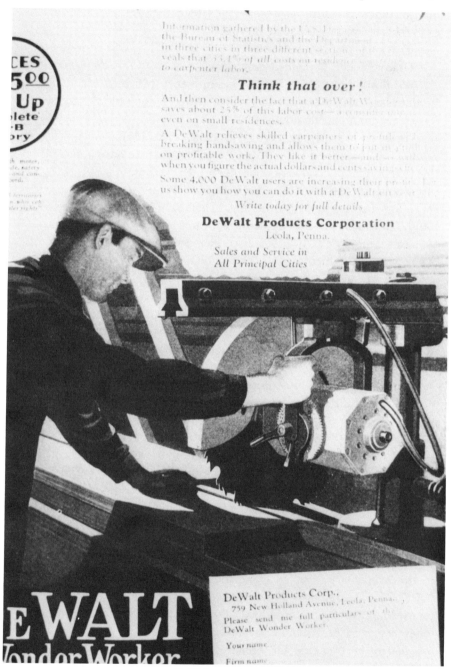

DeWalt Wonder Worker

month, that's all right, but forever, he [the carpenter] is furnishing the tools for his job. It gets a little bit touchy.

Grady Pinner, Berkeley Local 998:

We don't fight [power tools] because they run men out of work. In the long run, they probably make work. I don't think the power tools have cut anything down.

There's practically no cutting by hand; there's some but not nearly as much as there used to be. I don't even know if we have a designated saw man anymore. Everybody does their own sawing.

You don't see carpenters with fingers off any more. [You used to see] a lot of stub-fingered carpenters. They have learned to respect their tools. They make good servants but poor masters.

As a union we have never discouraged the use of safe power tools. We believe in productivity too. That's the name of the game.

Concrete work has got to be plumb and level and square. They use plumb-bobs. They don't use spirit levels. They use transits in long work. As a matter of fact, we used to have courses to teach the guys the use of the transit. We brush them up on some of the later technology at the apprenticeship school. They set up special hours to bring them up to date on their trade. Teach them to weld, and this sort of thing. When the laser beam came out we had to teach them how to use that thing down at the school. They use it to put ceilings in.

L.M. "Boots" Weir, Detroit Millwrights Local 1102:

There is an awful lot of millwright work in powerhouse construction: setting of pumps, coal processing machinery, pulverizers, setting of the turbine and the generator itself. It was rather clean jurisdiction when we first organized. You could handle anything that had to do with a conveyor, even if it was six inch rail line, with hand powered tools and a chain fall. Today they do [a lot] with a crane.

We were having to use power equipment to do the raising and placing of the [conveyor] parts. In come the Iron Worker with his argument over power equipment. The solution was a composite crew. There is an over-lap that has to be endured, I guess. I never liked that agreement. They began to preassemble great big pieces right after World War II. We had to be prepared for whatever development might come in the conveyor industry.

You'll never get away from the use of the hand wrenches, hammers, but tools have improved, small power tools. We used to do a lot of work in the field. Now it comes out already done from the shop. We used to assemble trolleys out in the field using little air-driven or electrically driven tools to assemble all this. A lot of drilling in the field, a lot of welding. Some of those things will never change.

Grady Pinner, Berkeley Local 998:

We tend to be somewhat more conservative than the industrial unions. We rely on our own skills and our own knowledge to make our living rather than have something that marries us to the job. Seniority doesn't have any place in the trades. We're a booming trade. We go where the work is. When the work is done, we boom out of there and go some other place.

I think the carpenters' trade will be around for a long time. It's true that they are designing around us, but when they were designing the power tools they thought they were designing around us too, and they really were helping us. I'm sure there will be carpenters around, people who are craftsmen and still have to do something plumb, level and square. If you can't change with the time, you're out of business.

Logic and practical necessity may lead the carpenter to change, adapt and adjust the way he works, but his attitude toward these changes, adaptations and adjustments is profoundly ambiguous.

Ed Cooper, Traverse City Local 1461:

[The work done by planes] I would say 95% of it, is all done by machinery now. You have your routers that took over, and it is all done by power equipment. You can carry a little satchel around that's got forty, fifty cutters that fits in the routers and the router can do pretty near everything that any of these planes could do, and do it so much quicker and easier. And your factories turn out window jambs and casings and the frameworks are all done on machines and there is no reason to have all these other types of tools any more. That's where the mill people come in. They do all that milling work so the carpenter that's building a house, all his stuff comes to him even pre-cut. Doors and windows pre-hung and all you need is to have the opening to place them in. That eliminates a lot of the time-consuming work. The house can be put up in a month, six weeks, where years ago it would be from six months to two to three years.

It's faster production all the way around. I've seen it in my days. I've even helped make some of the changes. It always happens: you find simpler ways to do it, and you simplify it in one direction and the next guy comes along and he finds another little gimmick to add to it, and he makes it a little simpler again. That's progress. You can't stop it. And I feel real good [about it]. It is real satisfying to know that you had the tools to do a good job and the tools today can do a good job.

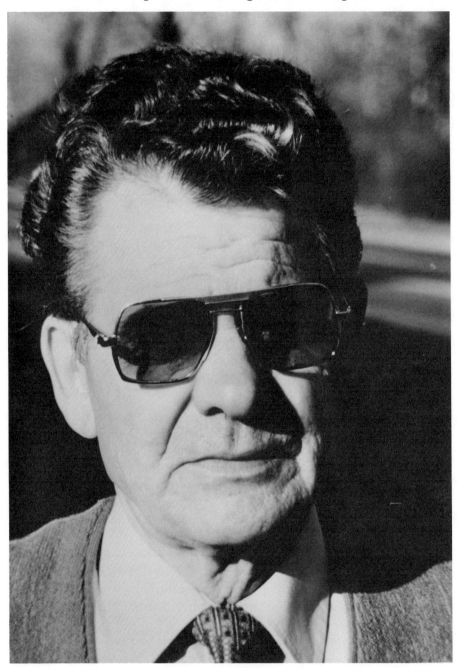

Grady Pinner, Berkley Local 998

Saves 25% of carpenter labor cost...

29 distinct operations can be performed on a DeWalt — with all the speed and precision of a single purpose machine.

A DeWalt saves money on any job

Some of them can do a better job, but the real craftsman that could do these things [by hand] is no more, because it is all manufactured someplace else and you just put it together.

The small, portable electric motor has caused dramatic changes in carpentry work. Today it drives drills, routers, radial arm saws, miters, and hand held circular saws. A few power driven tools can now replace the massive tool box the nineteenth century carpenter paid to have carted to his job site.

There were good reasons to oppose their use. They could kill the job, speeding up production so much that the job was finished quickly and the carpenter had to look for another job. In Elmer Swanson's youth constructing a house took months and even years. Recently in a special demonstration project in Alaska a two bedroom house was erected and furnished in three hours and twenty minutes. Power tools and industrial methods could create unemployment.

They could also lead to alienation. The carpenter owned his tools a century ago and took great pride in them. Elmer Swanson's lovingly recollects the first thirty-six inch iron plane he bought, and Len Zimmerman still has the two handled scraper the old Swedish carpenter bought for him. When ownership of the tools used on the job passed to the employer, did that not alter fundamentally the relationship of the carpenter to his work?

The issue for working carpenters was simpler: Power tools gave their owner an unfair advantage in competition for a job. An employer would prefer the carpenter who brought his own power tools to the job over the carpenter with hand tools. This in modern guise was the same issue addressed in 1881 when one carpenter might undercut the wage of another to get a job. Carpenters wished to compete on the basis of skill and knowledge. Any other basis for competition was unfair. Thus the carpenter never fought the introduction of power equipment. He simply asserted that this expensive equipment must be provided by the employer. He was able to enforce such a position because he had a union which negotiated such a provision into a contract.

Chapter VI
Working Union

Working union represents a personal commitment and a craftsman's principle. Both require the craftsman periodically to re-examine, to assess his practical achievements, and, if all is well, to renew his commitments. We have seen how individuals became members, but however necessary such individual decisions are, a union does not exist in the isolated act of a single individual. It begins when two join together, when one persuades another. As Wilbur Slye, Escanaba Local 1832, so aptly put it, "A lot of people believe that you should have your rules and regulations to keep people out, but that isn't the theory of good unionism. You bring 'em in." In one sense, it should be easy to "bring 'em in," for the central appeal is almost self-evident.

Ed Harper, Berkeley Local 998:
We just preached the benefits of belonging to the local unions [when we organized]. We could preach that they had power to negotiate for their betterment, wages and fringe benefits.

Albert F. Popp, Bay City Local 116:
[In 1931-2, Sears took over a store]. I got a letter from Sears to straighten out that job. They didn't want no non-union carpenters working there. Sears has hired union carpenters ever since. I was the Recording Secretary. We were down to twelve members, see, so we had to do something, or disband the union. I signed up about fifty carpenters there [at Sears] and that's what saved our union.

Mostly organizing required commitment, work, persistence, and courage.

David Charlton, Detroit Resilient Floor Local 2265:
The one I remember is Burt Callen. He was always preaching join the union. And it got him in a lot of trouble. He was fired here and fired there. When they found out [his union sympathies] he had to move

77

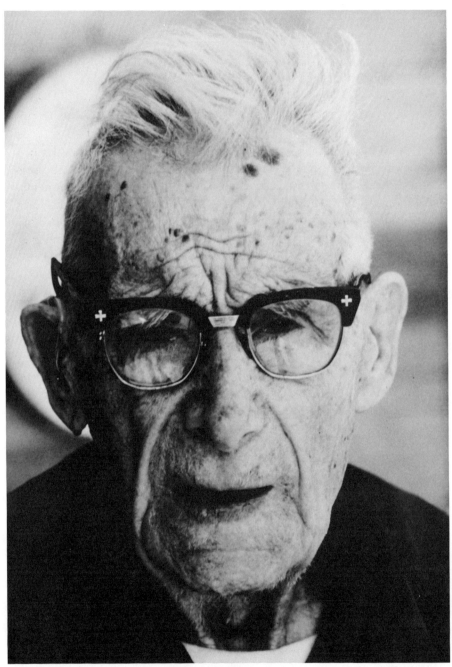

Albert Popp, Bay City Local 116

on. This whole thing started in Ernie Kastner's basement in 1933. There was about six of us started it.

Wilber Slye, Escanaba Local 1832:

We had over fifty per cent of the workers in that company. I was on the bargaining committee. We asked them to sign an agreement with us and one of the clauses in the agreement was that everybody had to belong to the union. We wanted to get a union shop.

I'll never forget. The company says, no, he didn't believe that anybody who had worked there for forty years should have to belong to the union. I spoke up and said to the manager of the company: "Do you know why them people don't want to join the union? You take that fellow that works partner with me. Old John. John's scairt. He says he's pretty near sixty years old and he's afraid that if he joins the union, he'll get fired."

He said, "How do you know?"

I said, "Well, I asked him."

"You mean you asked him while you was working?"

I said, "Yes. What's the difference if I ask him why he won't join the union or who won the ball game?" Those are my very words. I can remember them just like it was yesterday.

He said, "Mr. Slye, that's union activities on the job and we're going to fire you."

Hm. That kinda slowed me down a little bit. I'd done it innocently. I didn't realize that there's any crime, because I'm working with the man and doing my job doing my work, but I couldn't mention that dirty word while I was working.

So, to make a long story short, we finally got them to agree that these people should belong to the union, we got a union contract with them. I was a marked man.

[After the Second World War, I came back to Escanaba]. As soon as I opened my mouth at the [carpenters'] union meeting, they made me an officer right away. Although I was not working [in the trade], I was an officer. Then they made a Business Agent out of me. I transferred [from Detroit] into 1832, and they made an officer out of me. I have been an officer ever since. I have been retired for nine years and I have a special dispensation from the International to be the treasurer of this local, which I am quite proud of.

Ed Harper, Berkeley Local 998:

From 1948 to 1951 we built our membership up from 800 to 1700. We really beat the bushes, you know. There was an expansion in building in Oakland County. Mostly house work then. In 1952, Local 337 and

1513, the Jewish Local, were all the Locals in Detroit. When we started getting organized and growing, 982, 983, 1433 were formed in Detroit. Since then, in two cases locals have merged. 983 merged with one local and 1433 merged with another local. 983 is now Local 26, and 1433 is now Local 95. Also we had Cabinet makers, millmen, display decorators, and resilient floor decorators. The pile drivers are in Local 19 now in Detroit. Our territory, after 1032 folded, was all of Oakland County. Some of the Detroit locals got after some of our territory and we lost 900 square miles, thirty miles by thirty miles. I and some of the other officers fought it clear to the damn general office. Three locals in Detroit got part of our territory: 337, 982, and 1433 got a piece of our territory. Of course we still had a lot of territory left. We had everything north of the Eleven Mile Road.

Ralph Krimmel, Industrial Council, Battle Creek:

To a great degree [in construction organizing] you deal with the contractor. You try to show him the benefits of being organized. You can supply him with competent workmen and a benefit program that would tend to help him keep his employees and keep things more stable. In the industrial phase, you deal primarily with the people. You're out there contacting the employees and trying to show them the benefits of organized labor, of combining their forces to achieve the things that they want. I very seldom talk to a construction man that doesn't know that the union is a good thing. He understands that they set the standards.

Organizing is difficult anywhere today, because of the advent of anti-labor consultants that have no regard for the law. In fact, their teachings are to disregard the law, because the law hasn't got enough teeth in it to do anything to them. This is a complete reversal of when I started twenty-six years ago. You find them anywhere today.

Gerald Gavin, Detroit Resilient Floor Local 2265:

You've got to be so cautious about organizing people today. It's damn near an impossibility. Everything is a secondary boycott. All these stores out here, they don't hire their people directly, and pay them an hourly rate. They hire a guy off the street and say, "You are now a subcontractor."

So the guy goes down to Lansing: "Joe Dokes' Carpet Service." Where's his place of business? In a truck. That is it. You go to take some action with a store, and they say you've got to go take action with him. If you want to picket somebody, go picket him. Have you ever tried to picket a truck driving down the street?

Bill Potter, Detroit Resilient Floor Local 2265:

When I'm talking about, is when you could go and grab a guy by the seat of the pants and throw him out the window and throw his tools behind him and say don't come back here. And you'd watch that job and nobody would put it in.

David Charlton, Detroit Resilient Floor Local 2265:

See its against the law now to smash heads.

Ralph Krimmel, Industrial Council, Battle Creek:

The United Brotherhood of Carpenters and Joiners of America have had a substantial number of industrial people over the years.

Jurisdiction in the construction field is primarily geographical. They are given certain counties, half a county, that they work within as to the construction, pile driving, floor laying, millwright, etc. The jurisdiction in the industrial shops covers the people while they work in that given shop, and only in that given shop.

The biggest and the most primary difference is seniority. In an industrial shop, seniority is the key, practically, to everything. In construction, seniority has very little, if any, meaning at all.

Bill Potter, Detroit Resilient Floor Local 2265:

Tile and Style started up stores, man, they had them around here by the dozens. All over. They come in here and all they handled was tile at that time. Man they popped up all over the city, and there was no way you could keep up with them.

David Charlton, Resilient Floor Local 2265:

Don't misunderstand us. It isn't that we didn't try. Sometimes you didn't have very good luck with them.

Gerald Gavin, Detroit Resilient Floor Local 2265:

We more or less try to approach the [working] guy now. If you can't get him with you, forget it. That's the guy you've got to get organized. Not the store, but the man. If you got the employees, you've got the employer.

Leonard B. Zimmerman, Grand Rapids Local 335 and General Representative, UBCJA:

Organization in the construction industry is most difficult because the election process is almost out. The itineracy of the industry [prevents it]. Most of your jobs are short duration, outside of the Enrico Fermi or the big nuclear power plants, or something like that, if a job lasts six, eight months or so, that's a long job. Most of them are two or three month's duration. Under law, at the cessation of each building, when that last piece of work is done on construction, you've got a new project. You're not working the same project any more. The employer moves all the time and the people move all the time. If you got a hundred per cent signed up on that project and that project terminates before the National Labor Relations Board conducts the election, you're dead. You start over again.

We tell our people, don't go through the election process unless its a long project or its an industrial plant. The industrial locals we do elections all the time, same as UAW or anybody else. But for general construction, it is almost impossible.

Particular appeals may reflect these differences of work and organizational structure, and some problems of organizing never change. Some, like the credit system which seems to have no significance for the work place, have new and increased significance for the worker.

Vic Weiner, Saginaw Local 2585:

I don't care what kind of store, what kind of plant, they're all hard to organize. You talk to the average guy and he knows that he's getting kicked around, and he's afraid. He's afraid that he might lose his job, 'cause after all, he's in debt, he's worried about his family, he can't lose his job. He's not happy with the way it is, but he can't sacrifice either.

A case in point. I talked to this kid one time who was working at a store that handled carpeting. It also handled automobile parts. I used to talk to the boss because he was bidding on commercial work. He hired my people, signed a contract, I had no trouble with him. One day, I walked out to the car and [the kid] was right there. He said, "I got a problem. Can you help me?"

I said, "I'll try. What's your problem?"

He said, "I'm not getting paid properly here."

I said, "Son, that's out of my jurisdiction. I handle floor covering. You have to get a hold of the clerk's local."

He said, "I tried." So I got into it a bit. He was working 96 hours and he was getting very much underpaid.

I said, "Why the hell are you working for this guy if he's that way?" I was amazed he was that way. He treated my people good. "Why don't you get another job?"

He said, "I can't."

"What do you mean, you can't? Just take off one day and go look for another job."

He said, "I can't afford to. I'm so far in debt that if I lose one day, I get further in debt. And I'm afraid I'll lose this job."

Kenneth Johnson, Muskegon Local 100

I said, "What good is this job?"

"I don't know if I can get another job. Then what am I going to do, I'm so far in debt?"

I said, "Son, I never thought of this. You've taught me something." I been around a long time, and this kid taught me something. I understood how he could get frozen into that job and he can't make a move.

I lost respect for that employer. He still treated my people good, but I couldn't imagine anyone abusing somebody like that. [The kid] could barely get by on the wages he was getting to maintain his family. It wasn't so much credit cards and all. He wasn't that type. He was living in a shack.

Do you realize there's a lot of people who can't speak for themselves? There are a lot of people who don't even know how to look for a job.

The advantage of employing union over non-union carpenters convinces contractors to sign with the union. As Jake Michel, Saginaw Local 334 put it, "Organized carpenters can out produce the other ones. All [that non-union contractor's] got is one guy, and the rest are pounders. They're not mechanics. The jobs they do are no credit to anybody." This appeal, based on craftsmanship, on an appreciation of quality, of skill, today carries less weight than in previous times, and the need to organize and defeat the non-union element thus takes on even greater urgency.

Grady Pinner, Berkeley Local 998:

We have to organize to protect our industry and our benefits. You let the industry go non-union, obviously you can't enjoy a scale of wages nor can you enjoy pensions, vacation pay, and so on.

The union employer has to compete. It's almost compulsory that we try to keep the industry unionized.

You can't threaten to picket the job. That's a federal violation. You can picket the job, but you better be very careful what you put on the sign. You better make sure that there's a non-union carpenter there, 'cause if there ain't [one] working there and you picket the job, you're in violation. You can picket the site only so long as the trade is working there.

You can put the sign on that says "Joe Blow does not have an agreement with the Carpenters' Council." You can't say that Joe Blow is a rat. It must be a simple fact, an informational picket. Maybe he doesn't pay the scale of wages. "Unfair" can get you into trouble. That's only an opinion. You can put on there that he pays sub-standard wages, but you better be able to prove it.

It seems to me that in the last fifteen or twenty years that the trades have pulled apart. We don't have that cohesion that we used to have. At one time if you went out there and just took a picket sign out of the car and walked up to the job, they'd pop off it like watermelon seeds. Not any more. I remember a job, I had some non-union people working on it, I went out early in the morning and put a picket sign on it and there were deputy sheriffs out there. They were going around telling everybody that they didn't have to leave the job. And I remember what the shingler told him: "Up your ass. This is not the only job in the country and I don't have to work behind a picket sign. I'm gone." I remember that vividly.

Forty years ago, you never questioned a picket. If there's a picket out there, there must be a reason. Just stay away. To this day, my wife— if Detroit Edison is on strike, she won't cross the picket line to pay a bill.

Understandably, there is little love lost for non-union workers who may pose a threat to standards of craftsmanship the union sets. Moreover, their practices are repulsive to standards of decency and honesty the union strives to protect.

Gerald Gavin, Detroit Resilient Floor Local 2265:
You know, that non-union guy, he was a leech fifty years ago, he's a leech now and he will be a leech fifty years from now. He stays just a little bit behind you. The problem is, he can cheat the government, and cheat everybody else, and his pocket is ahead of you. This is the bad part of it. The good union guy does the things the right way, pays his taxes like he is supposed to, lives like he is supposed to, and he pays a penalty for it. This non-union guy, what he cheats from other people he puts it in his pocket. Now, all of a sudden he's on the same footing with this union guy.

[The non-union guy], goes out and gets a helper off the street. He pays that helper a hundred bucks a week. This is asinine. You go out and get a kid to help you for a hundred bucks a week, and you can make a lot of money.

Our apprentice starts at a total package [of] about eight bucks an hour. It costs [the employer] four hundred bucks a week and our competition is out there hiring a kid for a hundred dollars a week.

Vic Weiner, Saginaw Resilient Floor Local 2585:
Sub-contractors. Its just a subterfuge to get around paying Social Security, withholding tax, comp. insurance and all that.

Wilber Slye, Escanaba Local 1832:

It used to be that if you had a non-union contractor, all you did was go over there and put a picket up and none of the union people went across the picket line. He joined up, and there you had a union contract. You made a believer out of him. Today you can't do that. They put up another gate and one is a union and one a non-union gate. You're forced to work alongside non-union men, and it's degrading to you.

I was chairman of the union drive when they were raising money to build an addition on St. Francis Hospital. They had this drive in '58. I raised money from the different unions.

When we went to give them the money we told them that we would give them the nine to ten thousand dollars, if it was understood that they were not to use any non-union made products on it. This was during the time of the Koehler strike. I was working [on the addition] and here come a whole truck load of Koehler fixtures. Koehler was going to break the union. I withdrew the money. Told them I couldn't give it to them because they were using Koehler fixtures. We never did give the money, but we got a lot of bad publicity out of it: how bad unions were.

It seems that newspapers try to create a lot of public opinion against unions and you get a lot of bad press when you try to stick by principles. They get personal. I have been discriminated against many times [since].

Grady Pinner, Berkeley Local 998:

The press never was your friend. They never was the friend of organized labor. In recent years they have taken on a new tack: if you can't discredit the union, discredit the leadership. We've had some dirty linen in our house and it's been eliminated. I suppose there's still some dirty linen around, but by and large, the vast majority of labor leaders are honest. They may be inept, but they're honest.

You have the occasional guy, the racketeer and they give us all a bad name. Even the church has their baddies. And the police have their baddies, but we can't get rid of the police because they have a baddie in there, nor can we get rid of the church.

Ed Harper, Berkeley Local 998:

Right now we are in a bad, bad anti-union time. The big boys and the Republicans are not a friend of labor, I can tell you that. They're doing everything in their power to lessen the power of unions.

Unions are just people. Just good citizens too. [A union carpenter] is a citizen, a taxpayer, just a common person. He has pride, pride in his craft. He's proud to belong to an organization, an organization that has helped him and will take his part in the case of trouble.

Grady Pinner's charges against the press have merit. So much has been suggested in the press about leadership in unions that the average reader would scarcely know that unions originate when groups of workers come together to form an organization, and that commonly they choose one of their own from the rank and file to lead them. As a rule, unions are formed from the bottom up rather than the top down. As Marv Grisham, Secretary of the Michigan State Carpenters Council puts it, "you can only organize people who want to be organized." Leaders come from these groups and are chosen by them.

Ed Harper, Berkeley Local 998:

A union "boss" is just working for his local union. It goes by a vote of the membership on whatever is done. It's a democratic proposition.

I joined in 1924 and the next year they elected me president. Thirty years old and never run a meeting in my life. So I thanked them and said "I'll work for you and I won't lie to you. But if you burn your ass to a blister, you'll have to set on it, I won't."

L.M. "Boots" Weir, Detroit Millwright Local 1102:

My first elective office in the early forties could very well be looked upon as a popularity contest. I was just a young worker and we were organized, we were under a contract. I was content with it, but what went into it as far as officers' efforts to keep things functioning, I didn't know. I was nominated and elected to a minor office back in the early-forties, and picked up by appointment in late '45.

Marv Grisham, Secretary, Michigan State Carpenters Council:

My wife's uncle was the business agent. He got up at the business meeting and said, "I'm taking a two weeks vacation and then I'm going to the General Convention in Cincinnati, and I'll be off for three weeks."

They said, "Who's going to be business agent?"

He said, "We don't need one."

They said, "Yeah, we need one."

He said, "Jack Mahoney."

Jack said, "I just started a job."

I'm the last choice [for] business agent and the only reason I done it was because my wife's uncle wouldn't get to take a vacation if I didn't take it. I was laid off at the time. He said "Go ahead and take it, Marv, and you can be looking for a job. I'll be back in three weeks and get you a good job picked out." So that's what I done. I had a good job to go to when he got back.

When he got back, the officers of the local said, "Marv, you done a pretty good job. Why don't you stay on for a couple of months?" so I had taken a job for three weeks that has lasted thirty-three years.

Grady Pinner, Berkeley Local 998:

I joined in 1945 and in July of 1951 I came to work for the Local as a representative. I was active here. I was a delegate to the Council and I ran Bingo games to raise a little money, I worked on the Hall here when we built it. There's a lot of volunteer labor here. We built the hall in 1948.

Ralph Haines, Battle Creek Local 871:

When the '29 Depression hit, the carpenters that were not working on the prison job itself, couldn't pay their dues. Consequently the finances got awfully, awfully low. So I acted as business agent without pay while they were working on that prison job.

Jake Michel, Saginaw Local 334:

During the Depression when they didn't have anything, I was Trustee, Secretary, and I don't know what else, to keep the organization together. I held the Financial Secretary office from 1940 to 1975. It paid a little, not much. It was a part-time job. I worked all the time I had that job. I was in supervision.

Ray Skiba, Alpena Local 1132:

I joined the union in 1949. They elected me Business Agent in 1950. Of course it was a working business agent, for a while. Off and on, all of my days there was times that I worked part time. Demand was so great, especially at the Portland [Cement factory] when we built them silos. I'd work for the union during the day. At four o'clock I'd go to work at shift pile driving. I asked permission from the union. They gave me permission.

In a general way, the job of any business agent is the same, for he must deal with the human problems arising in work. They are always complex, for he must do right by the individual and by the union.

Vic Weiner, Saginaw Local 2585:

The business agent knows what the problems of a working man are. It is not his job to qualify a man to be a journeyman, it is not his business to inspect the job to see if it's a good job or not. If the Company wants to accept it, if the architect wants to accept it, the owner wants to accept it, that's up to them. He's there to take care of the interests of his people.

The union should maintain a reputation too, because you're not talking about [only] an individual. An individual is not the union. Everybody in the floor covering field in the jurisdiction of a particular local, is the union. He has that reputation to maintain for everybody. Now one [who] stole something, or he's a goldbricker and he's not doing the work but he still wants that good pay and all that stuff, is making a farce out of the damn thing. Right away, that's making a bad reputation for the union for everybody in the union.

[The boss], says, "Joe is putting in a helluva lot more yardage than you. How come? If you can't keep up with more yards, like he is doing, then you're laying down on the job and I'll get somebody to replace you." See, a guy like that [boss] forces somebody to work beyond his capabilities. In other words, I can run the mile in a given length of time. That doesn't say you can. We're all built differently. You have a certain speed and I have a certain speed. You may want to run the mile the same as I can, but you can't. You're not built that way, for some reason. God done it that way, and who's going to question it? But the employer treats everybody like they can do the job the same as the next guy. We believe [in] a fair day's work for a fair day's pay.

Wilbur Slye, Escanaba Local 1832:
I was out of work, and I had been a business agent, still an officer. I went over to this power plant they were building over here in Escanaba, and looking for a job. They said, "Sure. Come in tomorrow morning." That night my telephone rang and I answered the phone. It was a laborer who worked on the job.

He said, "Do you think you're going to work [the power plant] tomorrow morning, Wilbur?"

I said, "Yes, I am."

He said, "I can tell you right now that you're not. One of your buddies went to the superintendent and told him, 'Don't hire him. He used to be the business agent.'"

I didn't say nothing and went there the next morning to go to work. I got over there and the superintendent said, "Wilbur, we're sorry, but the steel didn't come in. We can't put you on this morning. But I expect it in within a week. I'll call you." So I turned and left.

He never did get that steel in, but the plant got built. It was another member of our local.

Another time I was the business agent and they were working on the court house and the contractor worked the men overtime and didn't pay them. One man came to me and I went to the company and complained about it. He said, "I'll pay them. Okay, if that's the way they are, I'll pay them."

He paid them their overtime. [Later], he said, "You know, I paid them more money than they had coming, to see if they would return it, but they didn't. I'll tell you, that if you were the last man in Escanaba to go to work, Wilbur, I'd never give you a job."

Vic Weiner, Saginaw Local 2585:

When things don't go well, my own family would say, "Why do you put up with it? You don't have to. You could go out and do better, make more money." But it's part of you. You must love it. God put you here to do it, I guess. I'm here by God's will to represent the people I have. The will within me is there for me to do it. I don't seem to be interested in doing anything else. I'm happy doing it. I've had my downs, but then I've always fought that much harder. It has to be a desire within you.

Wilbur Slye, Escanaba Local 1832:

One time my brother came to visit me. He hadn't been to my house for six, seven years. My wife said to me, "Wilbur, put those union papers and articles away. I don't want no union arguments when your brother comes. I want this to be a good sociable visit." So I stuffed my AFL-CIO News away.

After he had been here a couple days, he found this paper and said "Oh, do you get that?"

I said, "Yeah." Not much to say about it.

He said, "Yeah, I get that too. Do you belong to the union?"

I said, "Yeah."

He said, "I'm on the legislative committee in the shop where I work. I'm the shop steward." Then a smile come over my face, and I said, "we've got something to talk about in common."

It seems as though it was probably through our mother's teaching when we were kids. I always felt as though you was doing some Christian duty, that you was helping somebody else that was not able to help themselves as an individual, but through your strength of being united you could help your fellow man. I think that is the basic of good Christianity. I have another brother in Oshkosh, and he told me the same story. We never knew that each one of us was an officer in a union.

You find that people who are good union people are good church people. I've always found that.

What is a union? Its a group of people formed together for one common cause. That's what a union is. Is there any stronger union than a church?

Leadership in a union must reflect the wishes of the membership when a democratic structure prevails. What the union bargains for depends on the will of the majority, and thus there always remains more than one point of view.

Gerald Gavin, Detroit Resilient Floor Local 2265:

I think our real problems started when our big wages started. I can remember years back, we'd get ten cents an hour raise a year, for three years. A nickel. Back in their time, they were negotiating pennies.

Mike Belles, Detroit Resilient Floor Local 2265:

We'd be on strike for two or three weeks for ten cents [an hour].

Gerald Gavin, Detroit Resilient Floor Local 2265:

Then all of a sudden we started negotiating dollars. When we started negotiation dollars, (Belles: That's when I started putting money in the bank!) we started getting these big wages, (Belles: I'd come and tell my wife, we got a dollar an hour. She'd almost have a stroke.) the store owner then could get it done for half. This is where all the problems started.

Merlin Veysey, Sault Ste. Marie Local 46:

I've broken in lot of men. They worked beside me, drawed the same money as I did and didn't even know enough to drive the same kind of a nail I did. And they were getting the same money I did. This is one thing I had against the union. I come up the hard way. I mean really the hard way. Every year, I'd show them how to do the work and they wouldn't even join the union, some of them.

Whatever the trails and perils of leadership, whatever its rewards, they come to an individual as he begins his career through informal and democratic means.

Leonard B. Zimmerman, Grand Rapids Local 335 and General Representative, UBCJA:

I was the president of the apprenticeship class. I was more or less the spokesman for the apprenticeship group. We had some gripes about the apprenticeship class, and I would speak for the people. Anything come up on the union floor during the meeting and I was always there, so "let Zimmerman do it." I was very good at going to the meetings.

I had a suit and tie on and I suppose they thought "he speaks pretty good. Let him represent us." Acceptance by the people is what it really came down to.

The test of a union and its leadership occurs most clearly in practical situations which arise on the job. They may involve general questions of jurisdiction which arise through new technological development. They may arise over more traditional questions of a superintendent's powers.

L.M. Boots Weir, Detroit Millwrights Local 1102:

We were having to use power equipment to do the raising and placing of the [conveyor] parts. In come the iron worker with his argument about power. We were holding our own around here pretty well, but around the country they weren't. So the International presidents established committees that negotiated a composite crew on these operations. I never liked that agreement.

I felt that whatever might come in the conveyor industry, whatever development there might be, we had to be prepared to go with it.

Ezell Johnson, Battle Creek Local 871:

When we go on a job, we have what is called a Steward, He's appointed by the business agent. This happened to me. A job had been going for quite some time and this other guy was the steward. The business agent called me [where I was working] and asked whether my job was getting low. I like to make preparations for another [job] when I got one going. He said, "We got a little problem out here at the sanitarium. The steward on the job got fed up with the company. He's going to quit; you being steward out here would take a lot off me, 'cause I think there's going to be some trouble out here. The [superintendent] is kind of cocky, but if you can reason with him a little bit, maybe you can save a little trouble."

I said, "Sure." [I went to work and about a week later he called me in to the office with the superintendent and the foreman. They said,] "I think he would make a good steward."

The business agent told them, "Now, you picked him. I didn't. Johnson, you'll accept?"

I said, "Yeah, I'll try it."

About two months after that we were getting ready to do some brick work. The rule was that the laborers would bring the scaffold and the planks to the spot. We had to put up the scaffolding, hook it all together. On the other side of the building a foreman came to me and said, "Johnson, I want to tip you off on something. Laborers are getting ready to put up the scaffolding on the other side of the building."

I spoke to the superintendent and he said, "They haven't got much to do. Let them do it."

I said, "Uh uh. I don't want the business agent on my back." I put my saw down and walked around there to the labor foreman, and I said, "You're kinda getting out of your work. Aren't you? This is our work."

He said, "The superintendent didn't say for us not to put the scaffold up, so we're going to put it up."

I said, "I don't think so."

He said, "I'd like to see who's going to stop me."

I said, "Okay." I went to the office and I called the Business Agent.

The superintendent said, "I heard you calling the Business Agent. What's the trouble?"

I said, "Laborers are putting up scaffolding."

He said, "Well they haven't got much work."

I said, "That's too bad. That's carpenters' work. They can bring the scaffolding there, bring the planks over there, and the carpenters put up the scaffolding. That's the rule."

"Well, I think I'm superintendent."

"I guess you are. I wouldn't doubt that."

"I'm going to run the job."

"I wouldn't doubt that. The business agent will be here in a few minutes. You can believe that. If he says, laborers put the scaffold up, okay. It's all right with me. We'll leave it like that." The business agent came out and got the laborers off. After that, I wasn't a good steward.

About two weeks later the same [thing happened] and I called the business agent. I was no good for steward then and [the superintendent] told [the business agent], "I'm going to get rid of him one way or another."

The business agent told him, "If you get rid of him the company is going to pay for it, because he's your steward."

There's one thing that [the business agent] always told us: You know what your work is and you stick up for it. That's what the steward is supposed to do.

About two weeks after that [the superintendent] laid off all carpenters for one day. Then he called back who he wanted. [The business agent] called me and said, "He ain't going to call you back. I want to know what you feel about it. You know the rules. You know what you can do. Brown Brothers called me this morning and wants you to come back to work for him. You can stay off the job as long as they've got a carpenter on that job, sitting on your you-know-what. Do you want to do that? Or do you want to go to work? Brown Brothers wants you."

I said, "I want to go to work, for one simple reason. After the trial is over and we win the case I would have to go back to work for that same superintendent. I'd rather go to work." It was three months and two days before the trial. [We won].

After the decision [a company big shot] came over to me and said, "Now I want you to understand that this didn't have anything to do with your work for [us]. You can come back to work for [us] any time, and they *will* be calling you."

I was called back. The business agent couldn't believe it.

When negotiations break down, when work rules are questioned and the two parties cannot agree on an answer, the union's final power is to strike work. Such action may be forced by the employer or chosen freely by the membership, but the decision is rarely easy; the issue is complex. Even the strike as a tactic does not receive unqualified support from union men.

Ralph Haines, Battle Creek Local 871:

Today you don't see as many strikes as you did back in the strikebreaking days, when they used to send mobs in from Detroit to break up strikes. The company you were striking against would hire strikebreakers from Detroit or Chicago.

And it put the blame on the strikers themselves. I learned those things. I didn't know anything about it when I first joined the union. I never had a strike all the time I was involved in union [leadership].

Marv Grisham, Secretary, Michigan State Carpenters Council:

The way we got [our benefits] was by pounding the bricks. The picket line. Everything we got in this Carpenter's Union is got by picket lines. I remember back in the forties and fifties we had one year contracts and you could bet that there'd be a strike every year. The best thing for the union and the industry is a strike every once in a while. You get reacquainted. It also brings home to the members: if you want it you've got to fight for it. Nothing is free.

Roman Dunneback, Lansing Local 1449:

I had to take care of union business for quite some time. When it come time for arbitrating a job, or getting a raise, it was always quite difficult. We never had to strike, because I didn't believe in it. I don't believe in violence. We got fellows that don't believe in it just as well as me. When we was over to some of these jobs where there was violence, over to Ovid-Elsie School, two of us went there and just tried to tame fellows. There was only one little barb there through the day, when a hot-headed man was going to go through with a truck. He didn't. He pretty near run over a man, but outside of that there was many State Policemen and sheriffs. The union bought their coffee and doughnuts all day.

Wilbur Slye, Escanaba Local 1832:

[The union] maintains a stable work force for the benefit of the contractor. I suppose the contractor feels that workmen are like tools, hanging on the wall. You can call up and he takes one off the hook and gives it to you. When you get tired of him, you just lay him down, hang him back up on the hook again. Over the years they have kept this stable force of people for these [contractors].

Grady Pinner, Berkeley Local 998:

We have [now] a pretty good apprenticeship program. About ten percent of their time is spent in a classroom and ninety percent of it on the job. They are under the direct supervision of the foreman and the steward out there. They learn the moves. If they are journeymen carpenters and they come in here, they generally learn the moves, or they don't stick around. We don't enjoy a thing called seniority. We have to get paid for what we do and what we know, generally what we do. We have the right to drag up and the boss has the right to drag up.

L.M. Boots Weir, Detroit Millwright Local 1102:

They've outlawed hiring halls as such, of course, but we are a pool of men that are available to whoever wants our services under our existing contract. Which is a good arrangement.

Ezell Johnson, Battle Creek Local 871:

I'll tell you one thing that happened over there in Kentucky when we went over there to work on that powder plant. We could have forced the white local at Cairo, Illinois to accept us in their local, but we didn't want to if they didn't want us in it. There were segregated locals.

We was called—eight of us—to go to work a little place out west of Paducah. The government was building a powder plant. We went over there, and they had a house where the office was, until they got the place built. They told us to be over there at eight o'clock. We were there about five, ten minutes to eight, drove up, parked, and got out to go into the office there. A guy was standing there on the steps and asked us, "Where you boys going."

We said, "We come over here to go to work."

"Over our dead bodies." That's just what he said.

We looked at one another, and one of the guys said, "We was told to come to work. I'm sure we will work over here. I don't know whether it will be over your dead body or not, but we're going back to the union hall and we'll find out."

He said, "That's just what you better do." I never did find out who they were, but they were just stupid enough to think that they could keep us from coming on to work.

We got in the car and came on back to Cairo and told the business agent what happened. He said, "Well, you know how it is. Maybe they got a good point there."

[One of our guys] said, "maybe so, but I'll find out."

He said, "Okay, you find out."

We called the International and told them what happened. We called from his house. They told him, "I'll call you back within a hour." We all stayed there and they called back and said, "Those of you who went over there this morning, go back tomorrow morning and I will have some people down there tomorrow morning. Be sure that you all go back. Those guys [who stopped you] won't be there. You'll have no trouble. You'll just go in and sign up. That's all you'll have to do."

We got in the car the next morning and went out there, and sure enough, these guys were there and said, "Come in boys. We made a mistake."

I said, "I thought you did."

About three weeks later, if it was that long, the Cairo Local called us in and said the International is going to take our charter because somebody said we had refused to let you in our local.

I said, "Somebody *said* that you refused to let us in your local? Somebody *said*?"

He said, "Well the word got out. Now you all can join our local, if you want to. We're sorry. We made a mistake."

We said, "We don't need your local now." We told them we didn't care to get in the other local. We'd rather keep our own. So they agreed to it. We kept our own. That's what came out of that.

The power that comes with organization, the skill that comes from leadership arising from the rank and file, empowers not only the group, but the individual.

Ed Cooper, Traverse City Local 1461:

The contractor has got to prove to you that his method is better. In most cases there shouldn't be any objection to it. Either side should have a chance to try and find out. But if it comes out with the same answer, and one is saving bucks, I thing both sides of the fence should acknowledge it, if it is a safe and secure way of doing it.

In most cases [of conflict], I was always bullheaded enough that I could tell the contractor that there's a job waiting for me across the street. It didn't make any difference to me whether I was working here, or across the street. That generally licked the problem right there. I've never been fired off a job in my life. Never have. But I stood up for my rights, and most of them knew it. If I'm right, and I know I'm right, they don't lead me around by the nose. I just won't take it.

Ezell Johnson, Battle Creek Local 871:

We were living in Battle Creek. I had a car and all three of us was riding together. And one of the guys—Waterfield—his foreman said, "I want you to work overtime fifteen minutes."

He said, "Well, I live in Battle Creek and I ain't got but one way to get home. If the other guys—I'm riding with Johnson—if he's going to work overtime, I could work overtime. But fifteen minutes wouldn't be worth the working over, as far as that goes."

The foreman looked at him and said, "Well, on this job, when we say you work, you work." Just like that, you know.

He come over to me and he said, "Johnson, they want me to work fifteen minutes over."

I said, "That's okay. I'll wait for you."

He said, "Yeah, but he said I got to do it on straight time."

"That's not the rules. If you work over eight hours, you should get time and a half."

[The foreman] said, "That don't go up here."

I said, "It goes in the Local. It may not go with you, but it goes in the Local. That's the contract. I got back-up on that."

He said, "Well, it won't be in it if you don't work. He's fired."

I said, "Just like that?"

He said, "Yeah."

I said, "Then you fired two, 'cause you fired me." I went to the other guy and told him about it, and he told him, "You make it three."

[The foreman] said, "I hate to do this, because you guys just came from Cairo."

I said, "Don't you worry about that. We didn't come here walking, and we didn't come here hungry. Don't worry about it. Just get our money and that's it."

He said, "Well, you know that you ain't going to get another job."

He went and got the superintendent. He said, "There ain't but one guy, Waterfield, that's refused to work."

I said, "We don't' work that way. Ever since the war started we been traveling together, and we stick together. Everything we do we're going to do together. We ain't' doing nothing wrong. We know the rules of the local, and if you try to bend them too far, [we'll refuse]. Now, if you want to pay him time and a half, I'll stay here and we'll wait. But the foreman said we weren't going to get that. Now, what do you say?"

He said, "Well, we ain't been doing that."

I said, "You better start now, or you write out three checks."

He said, "I guess that's what will have to be done."

I said, "If that's the way you see it, that's the way you do it, because that's just the way it will be."

He said, "I guarantee that you won't get another job, not in Michigan."

I said, "Either you are crazy or you think we are, one."

He wrote checks out and the next day we went down to the union hall and were sent right out to Fort Custer.

If you violate the rules, you can expect anything to happen.

But if you go by the rules, the local would back you up. That's one thing I can say about our carpenters' local—I can't say about all of them, but I know about ours—we had three different business agents since I came to Battle Creek, and nobody's going to buy them. Nobody. They will stand by the local. But you got to go by the rules. The United Brotherhood, that means something. It just ain't a word, but you got to push it just a little bit. Just don't give up.

The rewards of working union affect one's self-perception as a craftsman, one's status in the group and society. The benefits can be seen in daily work experiences, in wages and in retirement conditions.

Ray Skiba, Alpena Local 1132:

The union gave me a lot of experience; it was all on-the-job training. Just about every day you ran into a different problem. And the living, when the money was there wasn't that bad, really. I get a pension from the International, I get a pension from the State Carpenters in Lansing, and it's not too bad. The wife and I can live half way decent. We don't owe anybody anything. The home is ours and if we want to take a trip somewheres, we're in a position to do it.

Bill Potter, Detroit Resilient Floor Local 2265:

[The pension] is one of the wonderfullest things I ever did see. The people that's leaving this local: there's got to be something wrong with them. I retired seven years and I never enjoyed myself so much.

The most important reward from working union accumulates continually to the spirit. One may glimpse it in the posture and the gait, in the directness and economy of speech, in the self-confidence generated by an awareness of one's own dignity. That reward no one can measure; it can only be felt.

Ezell Johnson, Battle Creek Local 871:

The biggest benefit I got out of the union, as a working man, the greatest thing was protection of your brothers. When you join they're your brother. Some people I heard emphasize the wages, but it's a whole lot more than that to me. It's a whole lot more in our union. As long as I do what I am supposed to do, nobody's going to run over me. I got something to back me up. But I got to do the right thing. I got to follow the rules. Organization is a wonderful thing. There are things that happen in our organization that I don't fully agree with, but it's the same thing in life. I never had no fear on the job that anybody would kick me around.

Chapter VII
Carpentry for the Nineties

What is the status of carpentry today? Does it remain a craft through which the skilled worker can find satisfaction in a job well done? Can the worker find the challenges and the opportunities for creativity the trade promised a century ago?

Cornelius Vox, Muskegon Local 100:

Carpenter work today ain't worth a hoot. Today my kids would buy a house and some furniture company would make the cupboards and hang them on the wall. That cupboard over there I built right there. I built the drawer, I built everything. Now that was interesting, a job like that making that cupboard.

Ed Cooper, Traverse City Local 1461:

If I had a youngster, a boy, that wanted to follow in my boots, I'd say No! I just don't think the trade in itself has got that to offer. If you were determined and that was going to be your gift, you aren't going to be stopped anyway. [There's a lack] in the craft itself. Looking back and saying I did this, not like a factory and all you done is assemble it on the job. Of course somebody's got to do it someplace on the line, whether he's back there in the factory doing it as a millman, or whether he's over here installing it, someplace along the line there had to be a craftsman to put the whole thing together.

Leonard B. Zimmerman, Grand Rapids Local 335 and General Representative, UBCJA:

I would probably [go back into carpentry]. I've enjoyed it over the years. Knowing what I do now and knowing about the industry today, I'd probably have second thoughts. It's more of a manufacturing industry today than it was in the old days when you were building actual stick construction.

Jake Michel, Saginaw Local 334:

See, carpenters used to do practically everything. When I was an apprentice, we used to pour cement, trowel cement, handle the steel beams—we'd handle them with these A frames and these pole derricks. That was all done by hand. It seems to me that the carpenter had more work than nowadays. We used to say that everything above the ground belonged to the carpenter, and that's what we used to do, outside of brick work, or electrical work, or plumbing.

The first year of my apprenticeship was mostly floor laying, but the second year was form building. We built the R. E. Olds building at Michigan State University. We rebuilt it after it burned down, only this time it was all concrete. In them days we had our own mixer. We didn't have-ready mixed concrete. You mixed all your own concrete. The carpenters helped on that too, pouring the concrete. We used to start at the bottom and turn the key over.

For years, the top man was always a carpenter, but now they've lost that some how or another. When we used to start a job, we would lay out the job. The next thing would be to build a construction shanty. That always was work for the carpenters. Nowadays, they pull a trailer on there. Before they do anything else, the trailer's there and the carpenter has got nothing to do. That's where they are losing all that work. It seems as though that old style: they'd come over from the old country and they'd follow the trades down. The Englishmen were plasterers, and the German end of it was the craftsman, the carpenter.

I don't know as I would like the way its running now, but if I had my life to live over again, and [carpentry] was run the way it was run before, I wouldn't change. As far as union, I tried to help them out like now, and it made me a good living and I appreciate it.

Yes, I would [go into carpentry today]. I don't think I would enjoy it as well as I did before when I joined, but yes, I would. There's room for good craftsmen yet.

Living today in the hearts of these craftsmen are the same values that moved carpenters a century ago. They assert a fundamental dignity in work, and even a special dignity in carpentry. Work should be done skillfully, creatively, and it must meet a high standard of quality. The doubts they express about the future of the trade stem from fear that these values today cannot find expression in their work, and thus even in their skepticism they affirm their values.

The threat to these values also remains the same. Are the trade and those who practice it becoming debased by short-cut methods and pressures to produce more? Can it be protected from "the wood butchers" P. J. Maguire scorned in 1881? Can a carpenter still find that sense of pride and dignity Len Zimmerman recalls: "On a trim job where we were working around an on-going facility, you'd put on white overalls and a white T-shirt. You always looked decent, neat and clean when you went into those places. You looked much better than in the grubby blue overalls, like you come out of the dock workers' local. When you're on a trim job, dress like a trim carpenter, clean and neat." Here echoes the tales of the nineteenth century master carpenter who went to work in coat and tie, who changed to work clothes on the site and who donned his coat and tie when he returned home at night.

Can the carpenter protect the quality of his life and the quality of his work from modern pressures to produce more? These were central issues in 1881 and remain central today.

Carpenters have demonstrated through historical example their willingness to adopt new methods, materials and technologies, rather than to reject them. They have demonstrated their ability to adapt to new developments as well, but these adaptations limit the craftsman's opportunity for creative expression. It will take careful and energetic leadership to protect that expression.

Anthony "Pete" Ochocki, Life Member, Detroit Local 337 and retired Second General Vice President, United Brotherhood of Carpenters and Joiners of America:

When I first started carpentry, Mr. Zako was like my teacher, as well as an employer. He taught me. Your employer was your instructor, particularly out in a small town. You had to have the ability as a young fellow to get along with your employer, you had to have the willingness to work hard to satisfy the employer, you had to have the willingness to learn from him, and to pay attention to him. It was technically the same as the apprenticeship program we have today, except I didn't have the classroom. That was provided to only the advantaged people, from the standpoint of locality, such as in the city of Detroit.

You get fifty miles out side of Detroit and we had to come up by the bootstraps. [The work] was everything that I thought it would be. Carpenters' work is hard work, but that didn't bother me at all. I was accustomed to hard work. I come up through Buck Haley's School of Hard Knocks. Hard work was just second nature to me. And the balance of it was very fulfilling. I liked being out there in construction. I liked the people in it. We not only worked hard, but we had a good time together, good fellowship. That made everything worth while.

I liked carpentry. You're able to develop things with your hands and your mind. You create things, things that have a very useful purpose, like to house people. I really liked the housing industry. [I have seen many improvements]. The fact that you're meeting the demand in a timely manner is an improvement. If you built the greatest house in

Anthony Ochocki
SECOND GENERAL VICE PRESIDENT

the world, and you put the greatest care in it and you had that for one family, when you got ten thousand families waiting for that house, then you're not really improving on it, 'cause you're leaving the vast number of people out there without something they really desire and that they really need, which is a home. When you meet the need for mass production in a good workman-like manner, and give them a good house for their money, I'd say that's improved.

New technology has to come into everything. You can't just stand still. You're either going forward, or you're going backwards. There is no such thing as standing still. I have never been one to put anything in the road of new technology in the field. I believe in looking at it, adapting ourselves to it, make it part of our craft, and using it to the advantage of the industry and the people of this country.

My uncle, although he was top line management and company orientated, he had a very definite feeling for the working man. He projected this: working people should be organized in the union. I just seemed naturally to fall into the union from day one. I felt that the working man was right behind the eight ball. [All he was there for was to] put his head down between his legs and just kept his back bent and work. I think there's more to work than that. I think there's a certain amount of dignity that has to go with it. If a guy's willing to work hard, let him have a little dignity with it. He's got a right to have a little break for a glass of water, or to go the bathroom. Back in those days if you went to the bathroom more than once in the morning, something had to be said about it. If you went to get two drinks of water, something was said about it. Those things irritated me. I don't mind working hard, but I like to be treated like a human being. This brought me around at a very young age to where I was very vocal in regard to what we should have as our rights as working people.

[After I got out of my World War II military service and recovered from my wounds], I went down and established my credentials through the local union. I started to establish myself in an apprenticeship before I went to the service. I was going to go back in and start from scratch, but they said I should take a journeyman's examination, which I did. I passed the test.

Back in those days, when you sat around during lunch period, there was an awful lot of discussion about your working conditions, and about your union conditions, and about your union. I think a lot more so than I've witnessed in the last few years. Of course I'm not out there much anymore, but when I have been, I don't find it to have the same kind of atmosphere that we used to have. When I got into the carpenters' trade I continued to pursue those feelings and those expressions. When I was a part of the local union I attended my meetings very faithfully, and I became active as far as voicing my opinions on the floor of the local union. Even before I could constitutionally be an officer, I was an officer by pro tem, by action of my own local union. I guess they thought I had the makings of something for the union.

My local was very good with me when I was a young fellow. They sent me to union leadership school, to the universities for the courses. They did everything they could to further my potential as a union representative. I feel as if I was literally trained to be a representative. And not to be one would almost be a betrayal of their trust.

The fact that I joined the union is no surprise and the fact that I became active within the union is no surprise to me. There is no question that my rise was very swift and very surprising to me. And the degree to which I rose is beyond all expectations that I could ever imagine. It reflects back to a policy that I have always maintained: it isn't always how much you know. It's your willingness to participate, to be active and to work hard. You can be a man of a lot of rhetoric and intellect, but if you don't have any initiative, drive, if you don't have that philosophy of hard work, you ain't going to go anywhere. And you've got to have that work experience to adequately do the job. You've got to know what you're talking about. You've got to experience it yourself. That's been my long suit. I like to recall the experience and then frame the decisions based on the experience.

[Organizing today is difficult. Years ago], because of the conditions that prevailed, there was a demanding need among the men for a union that could get them conditions and wages and benefits. Changes take place in the people, just as they do in industry. Changes come in the people who apply the technology that has been developed. In those [old] days it was easy to organize. We find that more and more construction work is being done non-union, [even] in a major proportion now.

The carpenter is a very independent thinking person. *Very* independent thinking. To the point where you almost wonder how they can have a union, they're so independent thinking. But they've had an organization for one hundred and two years and I would imagine they will have one for another one hundred and two years, in spite of the independent feeling. There's only independent feelings up to a certain point. They realize that they have to have organization in order to accomplish what they need to accomplish, for self-protection. Employers, particularly real oldtimers, really understand the need for a union for the stability of being able to effectively bid. They can bid on the effectiveness of their operating procedures of the company. The non-union element disturbs that whole stability.

The carpenter, because of being such an old craft, [had] a claim of jurisdiction which extended so far and wide, that the other crafts [as they emerged] had to naturally be infringing on him. A great many years ago the carpenter did literally everything. There was no trained craftsman [of the other trades] in the locality. When the country was young, the carpenter was the whole thing. They didn't have electric at that time, and you didn't have any plumbing hardly at all. The carpenter really was the plumber because he built the outhouse. Really, his claim of jurisdiction was established since the time of Christ! He also was the wheelwright. When they put up the grist mills, that was all done by carpenters. There was no iron worker involved. There was no electrician involved. There was no plumber involved. A carpenter did everything. His claim of jurisdiction was so broad that the other unions naturally have to conflict with us for their survival. We're the ones that constantly have to be giving up, giving up, and giving up, in order for the other crafts to feel that they are in their proper perspective. We've done a lot of giving up for the good of the industry, but we can only go so far.

That's why we are involved in so much jurisdictional [controversy] to protect our craft because we have given up so much already. When times get as they are now, there is a tendency to violate agreements and understandings [about jurisdiction]. When times are tough everybody wants to put their people to work so they even violate agreements that are written and signed between two general presidents.

Jurisdiction is a very complex, complicated situation. I am in charge of the Department of Jurisdiction as the second General Vice-President. We have a hot line staffed by two, sometime three people in the office—counting myself, four. Those calls come in from all over the United States and Canada where the local agents are not able to reach an understanding or agreement. Even a District or State Council could be involved.

Jurisdiction disputes have to be handled as expediently as possible because they can always break into difficult circumstances at the job site. Work stoppages, which we don't want to have. In some cases—thank god its rare—actual physical assertion of jurisdiction claims. There is a certain amount of urgency to the settlement of jurisdictional disputes.

Jurisdiction is really the life-blood of your craft. If you don't have jurisdiction over the work and if you're not staffing the work, then you've got nothing. Your membership is not going to be working on that type of work, which should rightfully be yours. You've got to defend it very vigorously against claims by anyone else. In order to be able to ensure that your membership is going to have that work to do to make his livelihood, and not have to join another craft in order to do what he feels is his work as a carpenter.

[For example], in the late thirties or early forties, a group of people who had been performing work for contractors decided that they wanted to become a union. In their mind it was questionable whether they should go with the Iron Workers or with the Carpenters and Millwrights. That was the conveyor industry. Those men decided that their best interest would be served by belonging to the Carpenters' Union. [A jurisdiction dispute arose] at the Willow Run plant conversion. That jurisdiction dispute was won by the Detroit Carpenters' District Council, at that time headed by Finley Allen. That decision stood for many years in spite of the Iron Workers claim that he should get a portion of it. He got a portion of it because of real physical violence that occurred in the industry in the city of Detroit.

International decisions [on jurisdiction] have to be recognized by the local areas. Local areas may develop some understanding through the years. Maybe it conflicts with the international and maybe it doesn't. When we make international agreements we try to say, look, this will apply with all areas except the areas in which local understandings are reached that are amenable to those crafts. So they exempt those by that type of wording. That would be done by our International and the other one, if it would lend itself to industrial harmony. We still exercise authority over the local areas on what agreements [governing jurisdiction] they can make. In fact, today, under the existing rules of our brotherhood of carpenters, no local area can make any agreement on jurisdiction.

Michigan is the cradle of the growth and development of the United Auto Workers right here in Detroit. They became a very dominant factor in the political arena. There was and continue to be certain animosities that developed between the building trades and the U.A.W. You now have a merged A.F.L.-C.I.O. statewide and I'm hoping that a lot of yesteryear's anxieties have gone by the wayside. There will always be a certain amount of friction between the building trades and the U.A.W. because the U.A.W. in these plants had tradesmen that they call the "skilled labor department." They are supposed to do the running-type maintenance. Big, mass renovations or remodeling, or reallocation of lines, and so forth, we feel we have an interest there and we should be doing the work. They feel that because they are in there they should do everything within the four walls. Naturally there's going to be certain conflicts, but these are going to have to be worked on in order to keep a united labor movement. They will have to be looked at with a great deal of realism on the part of both unions.

[We also must be realistic about organizing. Years ago], because of the conditions that prevailed, there was a demanding need among the men for a union that could get them conditions and wages and benefits. In those days it was easy to organize. Today we can't even think in terms of completely mass organizing the industry. We have to think of a very slow process of organizing Joe Dokes today, and next week we get Sam Dokes, and so on. We have to modify our desires, by the realities of things, and continue to peck away. How do you organize a contractor and tell him you're going to put him out of business because of your wage rates? You can't do that. You've got to organize with a whole different attitude today. You've got to effect a working partnership with the [contractor] you're organizing. You can't tell him he's got to pay twenty dollars when all his competition is paying ten. Again some of the desires of the union have to be modified. Some people call it sacrifice. To me its reality. We've never been able to get everything we want. You've got to have a partnership with the contractor. He's the one that employs you. He's the one that signs the check. He is the critical point in this organizing thrust.

You've got to continue to organize in whatever way is *possible*. You can never stop organizing under any circumstances whatsoever. Power comes only from two sources: money and people. Who has the money? The employer. So you either have got to bring him in as the organized or you've got to bring the people in in order to get to him. Its everything when you bring the two together. That's what our job is.

The union has created an atmosphere in which wages are high, even non-union, because they have to pay them in order to be somewhat competitive and satisfy the people they employ. They have to give them other things that's going to make them live like a human being because the union has already gained it. These guys, whether they realize it or not, are only getting those kind of wages because the union has negotiated for the union people.

Many, many of the non-union people out there are ex-members of the union. They may have a personal grievance against the union. What it really boils down to is he didn't really want to be a member of the union, he didn't like paying his dues, and he didn't think he got enough for his money, yet it can be substantiated that for every dollar he has paid into the union over a life-time, he has gotten six dollars in return. That's a pretty good investment.

History has a way of repeating itself, and will revert right back to the slavery atmosphere we had where they'd look out and see ten guys with a little paper sack under their arm and say, "Look, buddy, you either [take] it or I'll get one of those guys." The union is going to continue in existence. No question about that in my mind. There will always be a portion of people who realize that it means to the country and the future. There's going to be certain employers who understand it and stick with it, because under absolute non-union conditions, you have no stability in the industry whatsoever, which leads to shoddy workmanship and cutting corners. You give the employer a little latitude, and he gets the bit in his mouth and, boy, he goes. The greed of the employers is developing more today. They are starting to impose certain conditions on these working people that is not to their liking: elimination of coffee breaks because its costing them too much; they're not putting enough johns out on the sites to satisfy the needs of the people; they're not seeing that water's on the job; those things are starting to come in already. The employer is starting to push for that little bit more, that little bit more. He's going to go too far. The [non-union worker] will realize, hey, I can't do it alone.

As of right now, particularly in the State of Michigan, because it is probably the hardest hit of all the states, we could find that the financial ability of the Locals and Councils to function is seriously impaired. It might be necessary for mergers, for consolidations, and for charters to be picked up for the survival of the union right there in the state of Michigan. At this very moment. Our job now is to preserve the union so that it maintains its stability, and can stand the test of these times, to be the anchor that will be necessary. [Otherwise] they've got nothing to go to.

It is not practical to organize ten people into a local unless there is potential of growth that would make a self-sustaining local union, able to operate effectively financially and from a service standpoint. In my opinion, and under the constitution [a local union] has got to have a full time representative. That means they have got to have a certain amount of financial income. A local union is not worth a charter unless they have someone out in the field to service that membership, and service that contract that prevails in the area. A local of four hundred has an awful tough time and their dues have to get unrealistic in order to support a full time representative. It takes a lot more than four hundred to sustain a local union and keep the dues within reasonability.

[Consolidating] is a very emotional thing for the membership of a local union, to lose their identity by being merged with another local union. It can be very disturbing to the membership. So it has to be done with a lot of consideration. Mergers and consolidations should be considered on the basis of the need to do it, the reasonableness of doing it, the interests of the membership, the ability to service the area, the opportunity for the members to attend meetings, keeping the costs within the realm of reasonability, all those things have to be considered.

[A union] is the only thing a working man has to protect him in those things that are most vital; that's his whole being, of wanting to be treated as a human being and not subject to the indignities that I've suffered, even as a young fellow in working for someone. Yes, its helped wages. It's helped working conditions. But I think the psychological factors are even more important then the working conditions.

After I became a union official, part of it was in the office, but a lot of it was on the outside, policing the field. That kept me out in the air, in the open, where I could hear the birds and smell the flowers, so to speak, rather than being confined to hours of work in a factory full of smoke and dirt. Although I haven't worked outside, technically, for years, for thirty-one years, I have been doing what I consider that I am suited for, what I was trained for, what I was capable of doing. I feel that I'm in my right niche.